Supporting Children and Young People with Anxiety

This accessible and user-friendly resource will help a wide range of adults support children and young people with anxiety. Clear information on the nature of anxiety is combined with helpful ideas, practical strategies and resources to help adults feel confident in understanding and managing the emotional well-being of children and young people.

Supporting Children and Young People with Anxiety cuts through the literature and provides practical support based on sound psychological theory and evidence-based practice. Intervention programmes and suggested strategies have been tried and tested in schools and colleges, with young people and families, and can be adapted for use with groups, individual children or parents. Presuming no prior experience on the part of the reader, the authors acknowledge the challenges involved in recognising anxiety and delivering tailored treatment, and emphasise the role of prevention and early intervention.

All resources are provided as photocopiable and downloadable resources which can be easily customised for use with children and parents. This essential text will prove an invaluable resource for worried parents, students, teachers and carers, enabling them to soothe, support and empower the young people in their care.

Elizabeth Herrick is a Chartered Educational Psychologist, former Principal Educational Psychologist with Southampton Local Authority UK, and is currently working as an Independent Consultant with schools and families in Southampton and Hampshire, UK.

Barbara Redman-White is an Educational Psychologist currently working in the Cayman Islands, with more than 20 years of experience as an Educational Psychologist in the UK.

Supporting Children and Young People with Anxiety

A Practical Guide

Elizabeth Herrick and Barbara Redman-White

Routledge
Taylor & Francis Group

LONDON AND NEW YORK

First published 2019
by Routledge
2 Park Square, Milton Park, Abingdon, Oxon OX14 4RN

and by Routledge
711 Third Avenue, New York, NY 10017

Routledge is an imprint of the Taylor & Francis Group, an informa business

British Library Cataloguing-in-Publication Data
A catalogue record for this book is available from the British Library

Library of Congress Cataloging-in-Publication Data
Names: Herrick, Elizabeth, 1950– author. | Redman-White, Barbara, author.
Title: Supporting children and young people with anxiety : a practical guide / Elizabeth Herrick and Barbara Redman-White.
Description: Abingdon, Oxon ; New York, NY : Routledge, 2019. | Includes bibliographical references and index.
Identifiers: LCCN 2018029790| ISBN 9780815377191 (hbk) | ISBN 9780815377214 (pbk) | ISBN 9781351234580 (ebk)
Subjects: LCSH: Anxiety in children—Popular works. | Anxiety in children—Treatment—Popular works. | Anxiety in adolescence—Popular works. | Anxiety in adolescence—Treatment—Popular works.
Classification: LCC RJ506.A58 H47 2018 | DDC 618.92/8522—dc23LC record available at https://lccn.loc.gov/2018029790

ISBN: 978-0-8153-7719-1 (hbk)
ISBN: 978-0-8153-7721-4 (pbk)
ISBN: 978-1-351-23458-0 (ebk)

Typeset in Sabon
by codeMantra
Printed by CPI Group (UK) Ltd, Croydon CR0 4YY

Visit the eResources: www.routledge.com/9780815377214

Contents

Contents

List of figures/tables

Acknowledgements

The materials provided in this book have been tried and tested in schools and with young people and families. We would like to extend our thanks to all those who participated and gave us feedback on the resources. This book is the culmination of work with children, young people, families and schools and we hope others will benefit from the final product.

We would also like to thank colleagues and friends who have helped us with support, knowledge and skills over the course of the writing of this book. In particular, we would like to thank Glenys Fox, Adrian Faupel and Colin Woodcock for continuing to be inspiring wells of wisdom and expertise and without whom this book would certainly not have materialised.

Personal thanks go from Liz Herrick to Rick Brown for his never-ending patience, love, support and technological backup when disaster loomed. Also to Nicola Tyson-Payne, Rachel, Joe and Maddie Wright, who keep me on my toes intellectually, challenge me emotionally and give me the confidence and love that is necessary to learn and develop over time.

Barbara would like to record her love and gratitude to Nye and Carys, who give her life meaning.

Forewords

Liz Herrick and Barbara Redman-White are highly experienced and talented psychologists with a detailed understanding of how children may be supported when psychological problems occur. For the adults around young people – parents and carers, teachers, assistants and young people themselves – this book will provide genuine help in overcoming anxiety. Around one in five young people experience significant mental health issues and there is evidence that this is on the rise – anxiety, depression and anger can all be debilitating and impact on young people and those around them. Liz and Barbara cut through the literature to give useful and practical strategies to soothe and support young people and defeat crippling anxiety. Worried parents, students and empathic teachers and carers will make good use of this book and empower young people to take back control of their lives.

Peter Sharp, BSc, PGCE, DipEd, CertEdPsych MA, CPsychol AFBPsS, Freelance Consultant on health, well-being, education and social care. Former chief psychologist, director of consultancy and chief executive of the Centre for Workforce Intelligence. Author of *Nurturing Emotional Literacy*.

This useful practical guide to understanding and managing anxiety is most timely. The external pressures on children and young people are many; the incidence of mental health problems is increasing and troubling youngsters and their families. Teachers, assistants, youth workers and parents will welcome this book with a loud hurrah as it provides clear information about the nature of anxiety and, best of all, there are many helpful ideas and practical programmes. These will enable adults to feel confident in using tried and tested resources which have been shown to reduce anxiety in most children and young people. The authors, Liz Herrick and Barbara Redman-White, have many years' experience in working with troubled youngsters. This book is an excellent distillation of their understanding of anxiety and of what works when managing it. It is a much-needed resource for schools, colleges, childcare settings and parents.

Glenys Fox, Education Consultant and former principal educational psychologist and HMI, Ofsted, UK.

A little bit of anxiety can be a good thing when it motivates us to make that phone call or meet that deadline. In this time of growing concern over the mental well-being of children and young people, it is perhaps easy to forget that anxiety is a gift of evolution, a normal response to the presence of pressure and one which we must resist pathologising too quickly through narratives that infer there is something 'wrong' with the person who experiences it. It is absolutely right that more attention is being given to this and the other struggles that young people face on a daily basis. Youngsters today face unprecedented levels of pressure, from making sense of the overwhelming amount of (frequently conflicting) online information they are attentive to (issues of international conflict, terrorism, global warming and more), to the expectations of social media; from the ever-increasing demand that they achieve and succeed in everything that they do at school, to the societal pressures (which still pervade) regarding unobtainable body image. It is no wonder that many young people are struggling with the management of their anxiety. Given this context, this practical guide from Liz and Barbara will be a welcome resource to adults working with or caring for them.

Colin Woodcock, Educational Psychologist, Southampton City Council, Academic and Professional Tutor, Doctorate in Educational Psychology, University of Southampton, UK.

How to use this book

This book has been designed as an easy-to-use guide to help a wide range of adults support children and young people with anxiety. Some areas of the book will be a priority for some readers, other parts for others. It is not necessary to read all the chapters in order. If you are a parent, for instance, you may wish to start with Part 3; then, if you want more detail about how the school could be helping, move on to Part 2. If you want more ideas of how to work with your child, you could move on to Part 4. If you are a school leader you may wish to start with Part 2; then, if you decide to set up groups for your students, next read Part 4.

If your role is to deliver interventions to individuals or groups, you may wish to look first at Part 4. If you wish to deliver a workshop for parents, Appendix 4.1 provides a PowerPoint presentation to support this. However, unless you are already very familiar with anxiety and its treatment you are advised to read Part 1 before starting work with individual students, groups or parents.

All resources for the group, individual and parent work are provided as appendices which can be easily photocopied and downloaded as e-resources. The e-resources have the advantage both of being in colour and of being readily customisable for your use. This will allow you to create personalised resources appealing to the individual or group with whom you are working. We hope you enjoy the flexibility that this book provides.

Part 1
Understanding anxiety

1 | What is anxiety?

What do we mean by anxiety?

Psychologists consider anxiety to be an emotion closely related to fear. Fear is one of the five basic emotions along with sadness, happiness, anger and disgust. There is no single definition of anxiety, but some that the authors have found helpful are highlighted below:

> 'the anticipation of a future concern associated with muscle tension and avoidance behaviour'
>
> (Diagnostic and Statistical Manual of Mental Disorders, 2015)

> 'a nervous disorder marked by excessive uneasiness'
>
> (Oxford Dictionary 10th edition)

> 'an uncomfortable feeling of nervousness or worry about something that is happening or might happen in the future.'
>
> (Cambridge Dictionary)

Anxiety is sometimes described as fear, worry, unease and nervousness. Some researchers make a distinction between fear and anxiety. Fear is usually considered to have a clear object; for example, a fierce, snarling dog invokes a 'fight or flight' response, either staying to fight or leaving to escape danger, with the response disappearing once the threat has passed. Worry has a specific object which may or may not be real/present. Anxiety is often less specific, we may not know why we feel anxious, and it may persist over time.

Everybody has worries but anxiety becomes a problem when the fear or anxiety is:

- out of proportion to the situation or age-inappropriate (see Chapter 3)
- persisting for six months or longer
- interfering with the ability to function normally.

The Diagnostic and Statistical Manual of Mental Disorders – 5th Edition (DSM 5) separates anxiety disorders into three separate categories:

- Anxiety disorders
- Obsessive compulsive disorders
- Trauma and stressor-related disorders.

Problem anxiety will manifest in different forms, vary in intensity and duration and may include feelings of powerlessness and panic. Children may suffer a distressing level of anxiety without reaching the criteria for a diagnosis.

This book is intended to address childhood anxiety within the DSM 5 criteria for anxiety disorders. It does not address the other two categories of obsessive compulsive disorders or trauma and stressor-related disorders in great depth. Parents who are particularly concerned about a child and believe they may require specialist help should seek advice from a qualified medical practitioner.

What is anxiety?

Anxiety is a normal emotion which has evolved over time to keep us safe. The part of our brain that deals with emotions was present in our very early beginnings. When we lived in caves and were in danger from many physical threats, anxiety evolved to alert us to danger. As our brains have developed over time, the thinking part of our brain has become much bigger and stronger. However, these two parts of the brain do not always balance comfortably together. Sometimes emotions 'take over' from thinking. If we are in danger we don't stop and think about what to do, as this would take too much time. Without thinking, we react to the danger as quickly as possible to keep ourselves safe.

The emotional part of the brain sits deep in the middle of the brain and is called the amygdala. The thinking part of the brain is the outside part and is called the cortex.

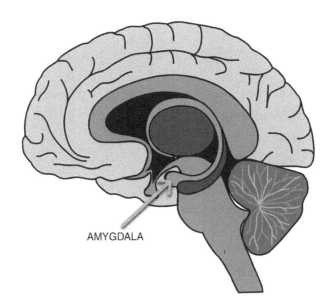

AMYGDALA

FIGURE 1.1 The brain

All our responses are made up of four elements; feelings, thoughts, behaviour and bodily reactions (physiology). These elements interact and affect each other.

Excessive anxiety is characterised by:

- Thinking – negative thoughts, with a tendency to notice possible threats too easily and to interpret situations negatively
- Feelings - frightened, fearful, out of control
- Behaviour – avoidance and rituals (safety and comfort behaviours)
- Physiology – extreme physical reactions which can lead to more fear.

Many anxious children overestimate the danger involved in a situation and underestimate their ability to cope. This leads to behaviours, thoughts and physiology which reinforce the fear. It is easy to get into a cycle where anxiety and fear lead to more anxiety and fear.

It is not possible to eradicate anxiety altogether, and neither would we want to as we need it to keep us safe. However, we can learn better ways to manage difficult feelings, challenge negative thoughts, and develop plans to make us feel that we can attempt things more easily.

It is possible that anxiety will be manifested in alternative emotional responses. It is not unusual, for example, for anger outbursts to be caused by extreme anxiety and a feeling of a lack of control. From an evolutionary perspective anger and anxiety are both responses to threat which alert us to danger, not just to our physical beings but also to our inner selves. Sadness, tearfulness and depression may also be seen as a manifestation of anxiety. These emotions can therefore appear together and/or alongside each other. We often learn behaviours to express our emotions that are acceptable within the family. Parents may need to explore these options when their child is showing intense emotions.

What causes anxiety?

The causes of anxiety are complex. Generally, researchers agree that a combination of environmental and individual factors affect the probability of developing anxiety disorders:

> 'Causation . . . usually involves a complex interaction of genetic make-up and life experiences.'
>
> (Freeman, 2012)

Genetic make-up

Studies looking at parents of anxious children and children of anxious parents have found that anxiety does seem to run in families. A person with severe anxiety is likely to have a parent or other family member with similar difficulties.

It is likely that there are two factors at play in this familial predisposition. First, there is an over-sensitive biological reaction to stress, triggering a fight/flight response when it is not necessary, and a general tendency to a high level of emotional arousal (Barlow, 2002). Second, there is a tendency to interpret ambiguous events as potentially dangerous (Eley et al, 2008).

However, it is important to remember that genetic vulnerability does not necessarily lead to anxiety difficulties. This will only happen when it is triggered by life events.

Environmental factors

Four childhood experiences have been identified as potentially contributing to the likelihood of developing high levels of anxiety:

- Trauma and stressful events; for example, bullying, teasing, parental conflict, sexual or physical abuse, death of a parent (Stein, 2008)
- Parenting style; for example, over protective, sending out a signal that the world is a dangerous place, not allowing children to cope independently with difficulties (Hudson and Rapee, 2009)
- Attachment style; for example, inconsistent and unpredictable parenting leading to anxious/resistant attachment (Warren et al, 1997)
- Learning from others (Gerul and Rapee, 2002).

Again, we must be clear that none of these necessarily leads to anxiety problems; they can contribute in some instances.

Short-term triggering causes

Children and young people can feel anxious about:

- people
- animals, birds, insects
- others' behaviour, opinions; bullying, for example
- places
- specific situations, such as tests and field trips.

Types of anxiety

The DSM 5 recognises and provides criteria for six types of anxiety disorders:

- Separation anxiety disorder
- Selective mutism

- Specific phobia
- Social anxiety disorder
- Panic disorder
- Agoraphobia
- Generalised anxiety disorder.

Separation anxiety disorder is the fear of being separated from the person to whom an individual is attached (for more on attachment, see Chapter 3). It is beyond what would normally be age appropriate, causes significant distress and interferes with normal, everyday life. It is characterised by excessive worry about losing the attachment figure (usually parents/carers), or serious harm coming to them. There may be a refusal to go to school or for children to sleep on their own. Nightmares about separation may also be experienced. Children and young people of all ages may experience this, but the onset is most prevalent between the ages of 7–9.

Selective mutism is a severe anxiety disorder where a child is unable to speak in certain social situations, such as with classmates at school or to relatives they don't see very often. A child with selective mutism doesn't refuse or choose not to speak, they're literally unable to speak. The expectation to talk to certain people triggers a freeze response with feelings of panic, and talking is impossible. The worry alarm is triggered in the brain, leading to a fight/flight/freeze response. Children with selective mutism are able to talk to certain people and in certain situations when they are relaxed and feeling safe and secure.

Specific phobia (specific types: animal/natural environment/blood-injection-injury/ situational/other) is excessive and persistent fear of a specific object, situation or activity that most people consider to be unharmful; fear of spiders, for example. Most children experience fears as they mature, including fear of darkness, loud noises, strangers and animals. Phobias differ from normal childhood fears in that they persist over an extended time and are not age/stage specific (see Chapter 3). Phobias are quite common in children and young people. Some begin in early childhood and some develop later in adolescence.

Panic disorder is manifested by recurring panic attacks. Symptoms can be very severe, resulting in an overwhelming combination of physical and psychological distress. They are characterised by the speed with which the symptoms arise and appear to be unpredictable. Very few young children experience panic attacks; these are more likely to develop in adolescence.

Social anxiety disorder is excessive fear of social situations, in which the individual worries that he/she will be embarrassed or looked down on. This may include performance-related events such as sports and music, or meeting new people more generally. It leads to extreme avoidance of social situations with peers as well as adults.

Agoraphobia is the fear of being in situations where escape may be difficult or embarrassing or where there may be no-one to help in the event of a panic attack. The young person may not feel able to leave the house and may spend long periods of time in a 'safe' place; a bedroom, for example. This is not usually seen in younger children but may develop in late adolescence.

Generalised anxiety disorder involves persistent and excessive worry that interferes with daily activities, school, family life and peer relationships. It is usually accompanied by physiological arousal which may include difficulty with sleeping. Children may worry about practical issues or their own abilities to manage; for example, school work, sport, or friendships. There may be accompanying headaches, stomach aches and the need for frequent reassurance.

Anxious children may appear to be worried about a specific issue, but as soon as that issue has been dealt with another springs up in its place. This is sometimes referred to as *'free-floating anxiety'*.

Theories of anxiety

Anxiety involves a complex interaction of thoughts, feelings, behaviour and physiology. Psychologists have differed in the ways they have seen the interactions of these components and this has influenced how we understand and manage anxiety. Four main theories will be considered here:

- Psychoanalytic
- Behavioural
- Cognitive
- Neurobiological.

Psychoanalytic theory was founded by Sigmund Freud (1856–1939). His approach emphasised the importance of feelings and emotions as the drivers of our behaviours. He made a distinction between realistic anxiety, which helps to keep us safe, and neurotic anxiety, which damages us. Realistic anxiety was considered to arise from threats in the environment, whereas neurotic anxiety is triggered by unconscious processes within. Treatment for neurotic anxiety centres on psychoanalysis in order to bring the unconscious processes into the conscious mind so that they can be understood and managed. This became the dominant approach to treating mental disorders in Europe at that time.

Behavioural theories developed later, and their proponents vigorously opposed psychoanalytic theory. John Watson (1878–1958) was the leader of behaviourism and for him and his colleagues all behaviour was learnt. For these scientists, thoughts and feelings were irrelevant. They demonstrated that we can learn to fear an object or a situation by a process called conditioning. This is when an unthreatening object or situation is associated with a frightening event. B. Skinner (1904–1990) developed this theory further by looking at the effect our behaviour has on the world around us. If the effect is positive we learn to repeat the behaviour; if it is negative we choose an alternative behaviour. As we have a desire to avoid anxiety we will naturally choose behaviours which reduce our anxiety. This leads to avoidance behaviour which maintains our fears, as we do not learn to manage effectively the things we are afraid of. Highly successful strategies for treating anxiety have developed from this approach, and gradual exposure is still widely used to treat phobias.

Cognitive theories began to be developed in the 1950s. Within these theories, emotions are considered to be experienced as a result of the way in which events and situations are interpreted (appraised). Anxiety arises from our appraisal of the situation, rather than the situation itself. For example, if you see a group of adolescents coming towards you in the park, you may think that they will be threatening and abusive, which will make you anxious and afraid. On the other hand, you may think they have a day off school and are going to play football together, which will not lead to anxiety or concern. So, if you change your thinking you can change your feelings.

The behavioural and the cognitive theories have both been incorporated into cognitive behaviour therapy (CBT). This intervention assumes that, as unhelpful thoughts, feelings and behaviours have been learnt, then they can be unlearnt with the help of a therapist. This is by far the most common form of therapy available for anxiety at the current time. Aaron Beck, who was very influential in the field of CBT, believed that people with severe anxiety not only overestimate the level of threat facing them but also have mistaken beliefs about themselves and their ability to cope with difficulties that arise. CBT has been very successful in helping children and adolescents with severe anxiety to change their thinking and beliefs and thus change their emotions (Stallard, 2009).

In the 1980s a group of therapies began to emerge based on mindfulness approaches. These have commonly been grouped under the name 'the third wave of cognitive behaviour therapy', with the first wave being behaviourism, based on conditioning (Watson, Skinner), and the second wave being cognitivism (Beck), based on changing thoughts and feelings to change emotions. The most influential of the third wave is acceptance and commitment therapy (Hayes, 2012), commonly known as ACT. Whereas in CBT thoughts are challenged as being 'faulty', in ACT thoughts are accepted. Acceptance is defined as 'allowing thoughts to come and go without struggling with them' and people are encouraged not to avoid situations which invoke difficult feelings but to observe and accept them instead. Mindfulness strategies are taught to encourage individuals to observe their own feelings, thoughts and sensations. There is encouragement to get in touch with one's own personal values and choose behaviours in line with them, thus creating more meaning and purpose to one's life.

Although clinical studies are in their early stages, results so far suggest that this is an effective treatment for improving well-being. Most studies have been conducted on adults, therefore knowledge of ACT's effectiveness with children and adolescents is limited.

Neurobiology has developed rapidly in recent years due to the development of neuroimaging technology, which allows brain activity to be pictured and recorded. Scientists are now more aware of which parts of the brain are involved in anxiety. The areas of the brain that are thought to play a major role in our experience of emotions are grouped under the limbic system, which contains the amygdala, the frontal lobes and the hippocampus. The limbic system is similar to that found in other animals and its job is to make quick, pre-conscious appraisals of situations and events to help identify which emotion, and therefore behaviour, is appropriate. Joseph Le Doux (1949–) has been at the forefront of identifying the importance of the amygdala, which is thought to be responsible for fear reactions in humans and other species. The amygdala is the specific part of the limbic system which identifies the emotional meaning of a situation. It responds very quickly, before the information can reach our frontal lobes where it can be appraised with conscious, rational thought. Because this process is unconscious we can be anxious or afraid without knowing why. The frontal lobes are helped to make judgements by the hippocampus, which stores memories from past experience. Anxiety is the result of a highly complex system which includes neurochemicals. Le Doux and others have considered it possible that when children or adolescents have an anxiety disorder the following may be going wrong for them:

- the amygdala is overactive, triggering fear reactions as false alarms
- the frontal lobes are not being active enough, so that rational appraisal does not reach the emotional appraisal centre
- the hippocampus is not giving the frontal lobes accurate information about past experiences, triggering negative appraisals when they are not necessary

Neuroscience is in its early stages and emotional responses cannot be reduced completely to physiological structures and systems. It does, however, show promise for our better understanding of anxiety in the future.

Models of practice

Solution-focused therapy

In the late 1970s Steve de Shazer and Insoo Berg developed the solution-focused approach to helping those with mental health difficulties. This approach was based on exploring the most effective aspects of a variety of different therapeutic approaches. This is a future-focused, goal-directed approach which highlights solutions rather than the problems. It helps clients to think about what they want to achieve in the future, rather than what has gone wrong in the past, and helps them to explore their own internal competences and support networks. This goal-directed approach can help children and young people to develop their own motivation to change and develop strategies that are relevant for them. This enables the child or young person to take some control in managing their own anxiety.

Emotional literacy

The importance of promoting emotional well-being in all spheres of life has become an area of increasing interest over recent years. Effective management of emotions is a necessary part of growing and developing as a human being.

Daniel Goleman (1996) identified five key dimensions that need to be addressed in order for us to demonstrate emotional intelligence: self-awareness, managing feelings, motivation, empathy and social skills. Understanding and managing our emotions is a key aspect of supporting children and young people who are experiencing difficulties with high levels of anxiety.

Motivational interviewing

Motivational interviewing is a counselling approach partly developed by clinical psychologists William R. Miller and Stephen Rollnick in the 1980s. These techniques are appropriate for clients who are ambivalent about making changes in their lives, as they can be used to assess and engage intrinsic motivation.

All the approaches above have something to offer us in our understanding and management of anxiety disorders. The interventions outlined in the following chapters have been based on a range of evidence-based research. The authors have found this eclectic approach to be effective within their own practice when it has been implemented to help teachers, parents/carers, children and young people reduce debilitating anxiety and lead fulfilling and enjoyable lives.

Summary

What do we mean by anxiety?

- Definitions of anxiety
- The difference between fear, worry and anxiety
- When anxiety becomes a problem

What is anxiety?

- An evolutionary perspective
- Thoughts, feelings, emotions and behaviour

What causes anxiety?

- Genetic make-up
- Environmental factors
- Short-term triggers
- Maintaining causes

Types of anxiety:

- Separation anxiety disorder
- Selective mutism
- Specific phobia
- Social anxiety disorder
- Panic disorder
- Agoraphobia
- Generalised anxiety disorder

Psychological theories of anxiety

- Psychoanalytic
- Behavioural
- Cognitive
- Neurobiological

Models of practice

- Solution focused
- Emotional literacy
- Motivational interviewing

Challenges to overcome

Anxiety as a positive emotion

The positive aspect of anxiety is that it alerts us to threat, prompts us to plan for the future and prepares us to take appropriate action to keep ourselves safe. This is necessary, as without anxiety we would not have survived as a species. It is often a helpful emotion; for example, if a child fears their teacher will be cross if they do not do their homework this may motivate them to complete it. Anxiety becomes problematic when it persists over time, is out of proportion with the reality of the threat and prevents us from taking appropriate action. A child who is so anxious to get their homework right that they are paralysed by worry, may not do it at all. At this point anxiety can cause significant difficulties in our lives, which includes our thinking, feeling, behaviour and relationships.

Normal levels of anxiety help us to:

- motivate ourselves
- plan appropriately
- enhance performance
- keep us safe.

Some worry is helpful

Excessive anxiety:

- paralyses us
- stops us doing things
- makes us ill
- interferes with our normal, everyday lives
- negatively affects our learning.

Too much worry is unhelpful

Details of normal anxieties at different stages of growing up can be found in Chapter 3.

Physical health

Each of the basic emotions involve changes to our physiology (body). Walter Cannon (1871–1945) first described an animal's response to danger as the 'fight or flight' response. Since then, 'freeze' has been added as a third response to threat, when we feel completely unable to react. This could have evolutionary usefulness, reducing the risk of being seen or heard. In the fight or flight mode our bodies are preparing to escape the danger that they perceive themselves to be in, either by staying and fighting or by running away. In all these scenarios the body needs to make changes. We may need to have a huge amount of energy to manage the danger, and heightened senses to enable us to detect further danger. What we usually experience as we get very anxious is:

- faster breathing and rapid heart rate – to ensure we have enough oxygen for our muscles and brain
- discomfort in our stomach and dry mouth – as the digestive system shuts down to divert energy elsewhere
- sweating – to cool us down
- tense muscles – ready for action
- raised blood pressure – to pump blood to the muscles, where it is needed
- pupils dilated – to let in more light
- nostrils flared – to smell more effectively and take in extra air
- eyes open wide and eyebrows raised to see more effectively.

When we feel afraid, our amygdala is activated and the emotional (worry) alarm goes off. This sends messages to the body to prepare for running away or fighting. To do this the oxygen in our bodies is sent to our muscles and the heart beats faster, ready to provide the energy we need. However, because the oxygen has been sent to other parts of our bodies there is less left for the thinking part of our brain. This means we cannot think very clearly when we are in a heightened state of anxiety. We find it difficult to remember things and listen to other people's advice. This is why it does not help to counsel your child or ask them questions about what the problem is when they are very upset. We must do this when the child or young person is calm again.

This energy boost, which is useful if we need to run away or fight, can lead to uncomfortable physical feelings in our bodies when it has nowhere to go. In line with the changes to our bodies described above, children and young people may experience and complain of a range of physical difficulties which can make them think they are ill. These may include:

- trembling
- sweating

- a pounding heart
- a feeling that there is something in the throat (which is where the expression 'my heart was in my mouth' comes from)
- dizziness
- headache
- stomach ache
- diarrhoea
- nausea
- vomiting
- breathlessness
- chest pain
- other aches and pains
- a 'fuzzy' head; lack of clear thinking
- physical pain.

Children and young people who suffer with panic attacks experience an extreme bodily reaction. They are overwhelmed with fear, and the physical symptoms develop extremely quickly. The person may feel they are very ill, having a heart attack or going to die. The release of the brain chemicals can often leave the person feeling drained and exhausted after a panic attack and it may take some time to recover. There is sometimes no obvious trigger for the attack, although situations where they are more common may be identified. Observing a panic attack can be extremely distressing and the symptoms may be so severe that those present are convinced that an acute medical emergency is taking place. It is not unusual for an ambulance to be called. The person suffering this experience and their friends and family may find it hard to accept that such a physical attack is a result of panic (see Chapter 7 for advice on how to manage a panic attack).

Children and young people who suffer from anxiety disorders that mean they have frequent episodes of physiological change may have consistently high levels of cortisol. This may then become a factor which helps to maintain anxiety over time. Living with severe anxiety can be extremely uncomfortable physically as well as emotionally, and may even have an effect on long-term health. It is important that we intervene as early as possible to ensure that children and young people do not suffer long-term consequences of persistent anxiety.

Our bodies are prepared for high levels of physical activity so that we can make use of the changes to our physiology. When we do not 'use up' the hormones we have released they can remain high for some time. Although adrenaline dissipates relatively quickly once the threat goes, cortisol may remain in the body for some time. Short-term boosts of cortisol are necessary to help us to recover from the effects of adrenaline. However, chronic stress leads to chronic cortisol elevation, where levels of the stress hormone never get a chance to return to normal. High levels of cortisol over time can result in:

- suppressed immunity
- high blood sugar
- high blood pressure
- carbohydrate cravings
- insulin resistance and type 2 diabetes
- bone loss.

There is increasing evidence from neuropsychology that physical pain and emotional pain share similar neural pathways and processes. As such it is very common to experience physical pain as a result of anxiety. Our everyday language supports this hypothesis; for example, having a broken heart, feeling sick with worry etc. However, the pain may create more anxiety and can be another factor in maintaining anxiety over time.

Living with severe anxiety can be extremely uncomfortable physically as well as emotionally and may even have an effect on long-term health. It is important that we intervene as early as possible to ensure that children and young people do not suffer long-term consequences.

Mental health

Effective treatment for anxiety disorders is very important for the mental and physical health of our children and young people. It is important to recognise what are 'normal' anxieties for children at each age (see Chapter 3) so that we can be aware if anxiety is excessive. Anxiety disorders persist over time (most children do not 'grow out of it') and have a negative impact on all aspects of the child's life. Sometimes adults, including parents, can unintentionally contribute to anxiety continuing, by taking actions that are intended to help but actually hinder the child overcoming their fears.

What might keep a child's anxiety going?

Maintenance behaviours

Four main cycles of thoughts, feelings and behaviours have been identified as maintaining anxiety over time (Willets and Creswell, 2012):

- Escape/avoidance – children may avoid or run away from a worrying situation
- Safety behaviours – children develop behaviours that they believe or feel will keep them safe

- Catastrophising – children exaggerate the risks and leap from one anxious thought to another
- Hypervigilance – children scan the environment for possible threats.

Escape/avoidance

The child or young person feels afraid, then escapes from, or avoids, the situation and feels better as a result. This leads to the anxiety being reinforced, as they have neither learnt that the situation may not be as threatening as they thought it was nor learnt any coping strategies. Instead they have learnt that they get a positive feeling of relief by avoiding the situation. This leads to more anxiety on the next occasion and further reinforcement of the fact they cannot cope. For instance, a child who fears going to school and is then kept at home never learns that they can manage school, and each day they stay away makes returning more stressful.

Safety behaviours

The child/young person feels fear about a situation, or has a worried thought, and uses safety behaviours which they mistakenly believe to be protecting them from danger. For example, a child may need to keep washing, checking, organising, tidying, counting, touching or collecting things as he/she believes it will stop bad things happening. When the bad things don't happen, the child may come to believe this was because they washed/checked/counted or whatever the safety behaviour was. Feeling safe is then mistakenly associated with the safety behaviour so they keep doing it/develop a habit.

FIGURE 2.1 The cycle of avoidance

FIGURE 2.2 The cycle of safety behaviours

Catastrophising

This may involve the child in interpreting the physical feelings associated with anxiety as a catastrophe. For example, the physical symptoms of a panic attack can be very distressing and severe. People having panic attacks may fear they are having a heart attack or that they are going to die. This fear of the physical changes in their bodies increases their anxiety, making the physical symptoms worse. Equally, a child who has done badly in a spelling test may think this means they will fail all future exams, never get a job, never find a partner and end up on the street, leading to an out of proportion reaction to a small issue.

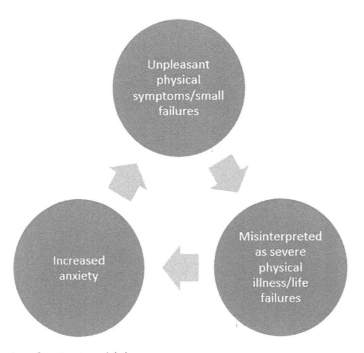

FIGURE 2.3 The cycle of catastrophising

FIGURE 2.4 The cycle of hypervigilance

Hypervigilance

Children who have suffered trauma and/or who suffer high levels of anxiety are constantly looking out for new threats. They check and scan the environment to see if it is 'safe'. We all tend to search for, interpret, favour and remember information that confirms our pre-existing beliefs (this is called confirmation bias – Wason 1960/1968), rather than applying rational, logical thinking.

Other factors which have been identified as characteristic of children experiencing anxiety include:

- negative, anxious self-talk
- mistaken beliefs
- withheld feelings
- poor social skills
- fear of becoming anxious
- 'payoffs', advantages for the child.

Anxiety has a tendency to feed on itself and create more anxiety. Managing to break the cycles above is an important part of the advice and support which you will find later in the book. For more information on these issues, see Appendix 4.2.

Parental involvement

It is tempting for parents to become overprotective of children who are suffering from anxiety. No parent likes to see their child in distress and will often find ways to avoid that happening. Unfortunately, this may mean that children do not develop their own strategies for managing the situations they find difficult, and neither do they have the opportunity to disconfirm their negative beliefs. If parents protect children from the situations they find difficult it could confirm the level of danger for the child. Too much reassurance can lead to an over-reliance on others and a failure to develop coping strategies. Strategies for parents to use with their children are provided in Part 3 of the book.

Summary

Anxiety as a positive emotion

Physical health

Mental health

Maintenance factors

➢ Escape
➢ Safety behaviours
➢ Catastrophising
➢ Hypervigilance

Parental involvement

Understanding child and adolescent development in relation to anxiety

How can I tell if fears are normal?

Just as it is usual for adults to have anxieties, it is a normal part of development for children to experience fears and worries. The specific focus of worries in children and young people is likely to change across childhood, depending on the developmental stage they are in.

Whilst there are issues that will affect how children develop through these phases (for example, developmental delay, illness, loss, separation and trauma), this chapter takes us through typical development.

For babies the task is to survive, so fears and anxiety are related to loud noises, unexpected events and lack of support for their basic needs to be met. Within the first year, emotional attachment to caring adults is important and so separation anxiety is seen when the parent or carer is absent. This is normal, as a human child cannot survive without adult support

Between 2 and 4 years of age, separation or loss of parents is still an issue but children are becoming more aware of other dangers and are starting to use their imagination. So this brings about other fears; the dark, imaginary creatures, potential burglars, for example.

By 6 years, children are becoming more independent and recognise there may be some real things that could harm them. Specific fears begin to emerge; for example, natural disasters, fire, animals. Often these fears are linked to the child's physical safety.

As children mature they become more aware of comparisons between themselves and their peers. Performance, relative to others, becomes an issue of concern. Friendship issues can also begin to emerge at this time.

During adolescence, young people need to feel they belong to their peer group. This is a very important part of adolescent development. They are also starting to consider themselves in the wider world and thinking about how their futures will develop. Fears of rejection by peers and academic and/or athletic failure emerge at this stage. It is common for these fears to be focused on physical appearance as bodies change and mature.

The following table gives a brief outline of what to expect at different ages/stages. However, it is important to remember that all children are individual, and children of the same age can differ widely in terms of their development.

AGE	NORMAL FEARS
0-6 months	Intense sensory stimuli e.g. loud noises, loss of support.
6-12 months	Strangers, separation from main carer.
2–4 years	Imaginary creatures, potential burglars, the dark.
5–7 years	Natural disaster, injury, animals.
8–11 years	Poor athletic and academic performance.
12–18 years	Peer rejection, the future.

TABLE 3.1 Age-related fears

(Adapted from Willets and Creswell, 2007)

We also know that some types of anxiety are more prevalent with different age groups, although again this an approximate guide. The common age of onset of anxiety disorders is shown in Table 3.2.

AGE	SPECIFIC DISORDER
2–4 years	Separation Anxiety
5–7 years	Specific Phobias
8–11 years	School Anxiety Disorder, Test Anxiety, Generalised Anxiety
12–18 years	Social Anxiety Disorder/Phobia, Agoraphobia, Panic Disorder.

TABLE 3.2 Age of onset of anxiety disorders

(Adapted from Moore and Carr, 2000)

What helps at each stage?

It is helpful to look at the normal milestones for children as they grow and develop so that our expectations of them are realistic at each age. It also helps to identify appropriate ways to support children and young people if they are experiencing acute anxiety.

Pre-school children

As children develop through the ages of 0–5 years they develop trust in, and attachment to, their caregivers. They will imitate others to learn their social skills and develop cooperative play at around the age of 3 years. This is a stage in which children's imaginations develop very rapidly. They start to use magical thinking and may not always be able to tell fact from fantasy.

How to help

- At this stage children are emotionally attached to toys for comfort and security and it is sensible to ensure there is a comfort toy available if there are known triggers for anxiety. Separation and loss of parents are an issue for this age group and it is helpful for some children to have a 'transition object' to help them feel secure. These can be comforters or toys, and they are special objects that give the child comfort and help to make the emotional transition between dependence and independence. They work, in part, because they feel good, soft and cuddly, and also because of their familiarity, which reminds children of the comfort and security of their own homes. It makes the child feel that everything will be OK.
- If children find it difficult to separate from parents it can often be helpful to leave a treasured object with them, so they are assured that their parents will be coming back to retrieve it (and them!).
- An imaginary friend, animal or super hero may be able to help them with their worries and anxieties.
- Visualisations which include magical thinking (for example, magic carpet, flying elephants) will be very attractive to children of this age.

School-age children

5–8 years

Children are now starting to use language effectively. They focus on facts, in the here and now, physical objects and literal definitions. They are developing ways to manage frustration and other strong emotions but still need adult support with this at times.

How to help

- Children need rules to guide their behaviour and will want them to be adhered to strictly. They may be very concerned with the concept of fairness and can often be heard to say 'it's not fair'. The consistent application of rules will support a child's security.
- Children are beginning to choose their activities. Setting clear targets and goals in small achievable steps will help children of this age to make progress.
- They will respond to activities that include drawing and physical activity. They are beginning to see the difference between right and wrong and will therefore respond to rewards when they do things well.

- This is also a good age to start teaching children relaxation methods as they may not be relaxing spontaneously in the way that younger children do. They will understand the concepts involved and enjoy trying out fun ways to relax, especially when done together as a family; for example, we are going to pretend we are rag dolls.
- Children respond well to stories they can relate to and may find it easier to talk about characters in stories rather than speak directly about themselves. There are a range of therapeutic story books available to support young children in managing their anxiety (see Appendix 4.8).
- Fantasy play may still be important for children at this stage and they may play out their fears. You can help them by offering solutions to problems that may surface in their play.

8–10 years

Children are now developing rational, logical thought and are able to see things from someone else's point of view. They are beginning to see that adults have different roles (parent, teacher, for example) and that they need to behave differently in varied settings and with different people. Children of this age are becoming sensitive to others' opinions of them and this can affect friendships and increase anxiety. Small conflicts can be seen as major disasters and become difficult to resolve. Encouraging your child to manage their friendships well and develop good strategies for conflict resolution will be useful skills now and in the future.

How to help

- Children of this age are able to understand the need for particular behaviours, so rules can be negotiated where appropriate.
- Children are moving from fantasy play to playing more team sports and computer and board games. They will be able to understand the difference between rational thought and emotion and start to understand the nature of thoughts. This is a good stage at which to suggest your child becomes 'a thought detective' (Willets and Creswell, 2007). They may enjoy considering whether their negative thoughts are realistic or not and challenging themselves to look for evidence. Board games which help children to identify their emotions and how to express them will be supportive.
- Exercise is very good at alleviating stress, so the more sport and physical activity your child is taking part in the better (see Chapter 8). They have more understanding of how their body works and will be open to discussing what is happening in their bodies when their worry alarm (fight or flight response) is set off. Helping to understand the physical symptoms of anxiety can help to stop the anxiety escalating.
- Breathing and relaxation exercises can help.

Adolescence

Teenagers are vulnerable to peer pressure and to feeling heightened emotions which are not being regulated by rational thinking. The worry alarm (fight or flight response) is likely to be triggered more quickly and more frequently during this period. Thus teenagers are more prone to anxiety, angry outbursts, tears and other emotional behaviours.

Early adolescence

Young people are becoming self-conscious about their appearance at this stage. This can lead to an increase in anxiety if not supported well. On the positive side, they can recognise and consider other people's points of view and understand how their behaviour affects others. They are becoming able to solve problems effectively, consider a number of different solutions and plan a course of action.

How to help

- Encouraging young people to become 'behaviour scientists' (Willets and Creswell, 2007), by weighing up evidence for and against the possibility of their fears being realistic, can work well with young people of this age. This is very helpful for young people who are motivated to change their relationship with anxiety. They are also beginning to be able to analyse themselves at this stage, which enables them to think more rationally about how they want to move forward. Young people's motivation to change is very important, however.
- If they want to make some changes it is important to involve them in creating their own solutions and plan of action. Obviously they will still need adult support to carry it through, as there will be bumps and bruises along the way. Imposing plans on young people of this age may not be as successful as negotiating ways forward.

Later adolescence

Young people are now able to think hypothetically and use abstract thought; i.e., have the ability to think about objects, principles and ideas that are not physically present. This will allow them to think about the likely outcomes of different courses of action without having to try them out first. However, they remain prone to intense emotions that are easily triggered and can change quickly. The emotional centre of our brains responds before a rational appraisal of the situation can be made (see Chapter 1). Understanding and managing emotions is an important skill to develop in this stage of development.

How to help

- This will be a stage at which a set of taught strategies (an emotional tool box) will be very helpful for those times when emotions are too fraught to allow rational thought to intervene.

- Young people identify with their peers rather than their parents and are needing to do more things without the family. It would be helpful to use this allegiance to the peer group to support your young person's difficulties.

- They may feel they can't talk to their friends about their anxieties, but being open and getting peer support is very important at this stage. Encouraging openness about the condition will help your young person realise that it is not something to be ashamed of.

- Noticing and recognising emotions can be supported by keeping an emotional diary/ journal.

- Explaining the difference between a broken leg (clearly visible for everyone to see and which will receive support from friends readily) and anxiety (which is 'invisible' but still causes extreme tiredness and distress) may help them to understand the need for being open with friends, or even just one friend.

- Mentors can be very helpful; for example, a football coach, Scout or Guide leader, youth worker. If they understand the young person's difficulties they can provide safe adult support, which the young person may be able to relate to more readily than with parents and friends.

- Exercise, nutrition and sleep are all very important at this stage, when young people's bodies and ideas are changing rapidly (see Chapter 8).

- This is a time when communication channels with parents need to be kept open so that teenagers can discuss their fears, worries and anxieties and not store them up to create problem anxiety over time.

- Negotiation will be more effective in allowing the young person to maintain some control and choice than trying to impose adult solutions.

- It is important for parents to spend time doing joint activities with teenagers, even when they do not look very enthusiastic. It is often easier and less threatening to talk to young people whilst doing other things together; for example, bowling, swimming, walking the dog.

The development of friendships

The ability to make and keep friends is one that children must learn as they develop. Friendships are important as they provide:

- emotional resources, giving children and young people the security to explore new situations, helping to alleviate stress and ensuring there are people to have fun with.
- opportunities to learn practical and academic skills and knowledge from each other and thus develop problem-solving skills together.
- opportunities to learn social skills; for example, sharing, cooperating, negotiating and resolving conflict.

Children with stable friendships are less likely to be bullied (Fox and Boulton, 2006), less likely to feel stressed (Wentzel, 2004) and less likely to develop mental health issues (Bagwell, 1998).

The following table shows the different stages of developing social relationships and how to help at each stage.

AGE	DEVELOPMENTAL LEVEL	HOW TO HELP
Age 3–7	Momentary playmates – a friend is someone you play with or alongside.	Offer plenty of social opportunities, play groups, nursery, play dates and school.
Age 4–9	One-way assistance – a friend is someone who helps you out.	Help children understand and practise turn taking, sharing, fairness.
Age 6–12	Fair weather cooperation – a friendship involves helping each other out. Friendships may be vulnerable and easily broken by minor setbacks or conflicts.	Discuss respect, cooperation, how to manage conflict and how to repair relationships.
Age 9–15	Intimate friendships – involves intimacy and mutuality. Friendships will last despite setbacks and conflicts.	Help children develop tolerance, understanding of diversity and other people's perspectives.
Age 12+	Autonomous interdependence – friendships grow and change with time. A friend is not possessive and recognises their own and others' needs to have other relationships.	Help young people understand how to manage friendships in a group, learn to be welcoming to others and not possessive (exclusive) in their friendships.

TABLE 3.3 Stages of friendship development

(Stages based on Selmon and Jaquette, 1977)

Conclusion

This chapter has looked in some detail at developmental stages, associated risks and strategies of support. It is important to recognise, however, that the age groups overlap, and children will move in and out of different stages as they mature. Learning is not a linear process but involves three steps forward and two back over extended periods of time.

It is important to support children with their skills at the developmental stage that they are presenting with, rather than their chronological age.

Summary

Normal fears and anxieties

Age of onset of problem anxiety

How to help children with anxiety as they develop

➤ Pre-school
➤ School age
  • 5–8 years
  • 8–10 years
➤ Early adolescence
➤ Later adolescence

The development of friendships

Conclusion

Part 2
Managing anxiety at school

Whole-school support

It is important for schools to support and promote emotional well-being and mental health, and to provide the optimum conditions for academic achievement. Schools are where the vast majority of children spend much of their time for more than a decade, so they can make a substantial contribution to emotional well-being and mental health. (Rutter, 1979).

Schools have a profound influence on students. We all have stories to tell about incidents in our own lives that happened at school, both good and bad, and how they shaped us. Whilst children's emotional development is influenced by many factors, ranging from immediate close family to widely held community beliefs and practices, the school environment is key. The implicit messages a child receives from within the school community can have an enormous influence on their well-being.

Leadership, values and aims

Effective schools

Ten characteristics of effective schools have been identified by the National Commission on Education (1996). They are summarised below and encapsulate the discussion in this chapter:

1. Strong leadership by the head teacher
2. Good atmosphere from shared values and attractive environment
3. High expectations of pupils
4. Clear focus on teaching and learning
5. Good assessment of pupils
6. Pupils share responsibility for learning
7. Pupils participate in the life of the school
8. Incentives for pupils to succeed
9. Parental involvement
10. Extracurricular activities to broaden pupils' interests and build good relationships in school.

Ethos and values

The ethos of the school concerns the values and beliefs of the school community that underpin custom and practice throughout the school. School managers need to be clear what their core values and beliefs are and ensure that all the staff and governors agree and sign up to them. The ethos and vision of the school should promote emotional security and ensure that all staff and pupils feel they are respected.

Policies can then be developed in line with core values and beliefs. These values will influence a range of practices, including management style, relationships between staff, relationships between pupils and staff, behaviour support, pastoral care plans, communication with parents, working with the wider community, pupil participation and styles of teaching.

The importance of policies

Some may feel that policies are a waste of time and, whilst needing to be completed for inspection purposes, have little relevance to everyday practice. However, if a policy has been developed by governors, parents, teaching and non-teaching staff, is communicated well and is monitored and reviewed regularly, it becomes a dynamic set of procedural and practice guidelines which support all those working in the school for the benefit of the students.

Although there is no statutory requirement, a number of schools are now developing a mental health and well-being policy. An example of good practice has been developed by the Charlie Waller Memorial Trust (see Useful websites) and provides excellent support for schools.

There is statutory guidance about the support that pupils with medical conditions should receive and a requirement that schools have a clear SEND (special educational needs and disabilities) policy. This should outline the support available for children who are having social, emotional and mental health difficulties (SEMH). SEND information is required to be published on a school's website.

For pupils and staff to feel safe at school there must be clear guidance on managing pupil behaviour and bullying. Behaviour and anti-bullying policies will need to take account of the needs of children with mental health issues as well as those with behavioural problems.

A school is also required to make 'reasonable adjustments' in order that children with disabilities are not disadvantaged.

Ensuring that the policies link with each other and provide a coherent message which reflects the school's ethos and values is key to effective practice.

Systems and practices

Relationship-building and pastoral care

> 'Social connection is the bread and butter of human life and rejection strikes at its very core.'

> (Baumeister, 2005)

Building good relationships and maintaining high expectations for all students is of vital importance. This includes:

> 'practices that encourage feelings of emotional security and the development of high self-esteem based on trusting and supportive educational relationships.'

> (Cooper and Cefai, 2009)

Belonging is a fundamental human need. As Maslow's hierarchy of need suggests (see Chapter 8), after our physical needs are met – i.e., air, food, rest, shelter – our safety needs are the next most important for us, including protection against danger, threat and freedom from fear. This can be problematic for highly anxious children as they perceive danger far more readily and do not feel free from threat or fear. The importance of belonging (i.e., being accepted, giving and receiving love and friendship) follows in the hierarchy, with only physical needs and safety being more important. As adults we can usually choose to be with people and in groups that we feel we belong to. When children and young people are at school they have more limited choices either of groups to join or groups to avoid.

The sense of belonging to the school community is fostered by the development of supportive and trusting relationships. Trusting and supportive relationships between pupils and staff, and with parents, encourage the development of belonging to the school community for all involved. Involving pupils in feeling that their opinions will be respected and understood can be established through pupil councils.

Whole School Quality Circle Time, devised by Jenny Mosley, is a process for improving communication and emotional and social skills, which she describes as:

> 'a democratic and practical school management system which addresses social, emotional and behavioural issues through a systemic approach.'

There are many other ways to promote pupil involvement, including peer mediation, peer tutoring, peer mentoring, school councils, questionnaires for feedback etc. The advent of nurture groups in some primary schools allows children to develop their emotional and social skills in a safe and non-judgemental environment. The safer children feel emotionally the more able they feel to take appropriate risks and develop emotional resilience. These factors will improve learning and promote good academic achievement, as well as reducing the likelihood of children becoming overly anxious in the school environment. The importance of listening to children and young people is discussed further in Chapter 5.

We know that children are affected by the anxiety experienced by adults, and that adults, like children, are susceptible to emotional hijacking; i.e., emotional responses and behaviours instead of rational thoughts, especially when they are stressed. It is important, therefore, that staff also feel emotionally supported in the workplace and that there are systems in place to support staff who are feeling stressed in their job or concerned about particular children.

The effectiveness of the pastoral care system is crucial in supporting children and young people's mental health, well-being and academic development. It should be inextricably linked with teaching and learning and the structural organisation of the school. It needs to promote students' personal and social development. This is done through the quality of teaching and learning; the nature of relationships among pupils, teachers and non-teaching staff; arrangements for monitoring pupils' overall progress (academic, personal and social); specific pastoral and support systems; and through extra-curricular activities (Her Majesty's Inspectors of Schools, 1989).

Effective pastoral care can assist students to develop positive self-esteem, healthy risk taking, goal setting and negotiation skills. These skills are known to enhance students' strengths and resilience over time (Nadge, 2005).

Quality pastoral care focuses on the whole student (personal, social and academic) and engages all members of the school community as providers of pastoral care.

Careful monitoring and reviewing of the pastoral care system can ensure all students are equally supported both academically and socially.

A ten-point plan for developing pastoral care systems (Cross and Lester, 2014) can be found online.

Curriculum

Whilst British schools are still bound to follow the National Curriculum, there is now some flexibility. A diverse and creative curriculum that encourages pupils to maintain their engagement with learning is crucial to good attendance, good behaviour and motivation to learn.

Personal, social and health education

A personal, social and health curriculum which includes support for understanding mental health issues should be in place in schools. Guidance for schools on preparing to teach about mental health and emotional well-being have been produced by the PSHE Association (2017). Lesson plans are also provided which span key stages 1–4 (5–16 years).

Special educational needs and disabilities

A mental health condition such as anxiety is considered a disability if:

> 'it has a long-term effect on your day to day activity.'
>
> (Equality Act, 2010)

Children experiencing special educational needs and disabilities (SEND) are likely to need the curriculum to be adapted for their needs. It is important that all staff are aware of the importance of high-quality universal teaching in the first instance. If a child or young person has specific needs (for example, dyslexia, attention deficit disorder, autistic spectrum disorder), there should be information readily available for staff to understand the strengths and difficulties associated with each condition. They should also have access to support for adapting the curriculum and using specific strategies in the classroom. This would typically be supported by the special educational needs coordinator (SENCo).

Differentiation

Careful differentiation of the curriculum is vital to optimise each pupil's learning potential. For example, reading and spelling levels must be considered when providing worksheets, and appropriate levels of structure and scaffolding will be necessary for learners who need to work in small steps. Difficulties in learning to read or write can cause anxiety in children and their parents. Children with SEND often work with teaching assistants. It is important that this is carefully managed and supervised by the class teacher and the SENCo. Recent research on the effective use of teaching assistants has been published (Webster and Russell, 2015) which makes it clear that they need to be thoughtfully deployed and have sufficient training to understand the best way to work with children. It is all too easy for a child to become dependent on adult help and for the adult helper to 'do it for' the child. This will not lead to independent learning, academic progress or confidence building.

Anxious children and young people

Children and young people showing signs of anxiety may need specific adaptations to their timetables and the curriculum they follow. For some it may be helpful to allow them to work privately for some tasks. There may be specific lessons or topics that cause the pupil anxiety, or it may be that unstructured time in the playground or specific situations (changing for PE, for example) lead to anxiety. It is important to sit down with the pupil and parents to establish the triggers and identify strategies to support the pupil whilst ensuring that the anxiety is not inadvertently being maintained (see Chapter 2). Referring to the school's mental health strategy and ensuring a consistent approach across the school will be important. The positive effects of exercise, music, dance and sport on mental health will be discussed further in Chapter 8.

Physical environment

Spending time and energy on the physical environment of your school can make a big difference to pupil and staff attitudes towards their school. For example, the use of carpets and other soft furnishings significantly reduces noise levels and 'humanises' the school setting, which in turn tends to improve behaviour. This can be particularly beneficial to children who have sensory or attention difficulties, as high levels of noise and some specific noises can be distressing and distracting. It is difficult for some children to 'ignore' surrounding noise.

Better school grounds have also been found to create better-behaved children and reduce bullying and vandalism (Learning through Landscapes, 2003). School grounds not only offer areas for play and sports, they may also provide opportunities for children to learn about insects, birds and plants, which can stimulate further study in these areas. A good quality environment

> 'gives pupils a feel-good factor, which is bound to lead to better academic performance'.
>
> (Hart, 2003)

Studies by the National Foundation for Educational Research found clear associations with improved physical school environments and an improvement in attitudes to, and well-being in, the school (Rudd et al., 2008).

Clearly budgets are tight but, even on a tight budget, improvements to the physical environment of a school are likely to have a positive impact, especially if the pupils are involved in some of the changes.

Working with others

Working with parents/carers

All schools should take active steps to engage parents in pupils' learning.

It is a fact that not all parents feel comfortable coming in to school and that trust needs to be built. However, almost all parents care deeply about their children's education and want their status as school stakeholders to be recognised and appreciated.

Schools that provide family learning enable parents and children to spend time together, with supervision, on activities such as homework, clubs and study days. Evaluation shows that in projects that deliver adult learning, parents reported a positive effect on their perception of themselves as learners and their ability to support their child. Parents also benefit from the improved behaviour and social skills of their child. Family learning programmes often provide the first step for parents towards adult education or basic skills training. They also have a very positive impact on the performance of pupils.

Providing a range of activities and services enables schools to develop closer relationships with pupils' families. Working parents may value the opportunities for involvement in the school community provided by extended opening hours or evening meetings. Schools that offer pre-school activities and childcare provision have also found them useful in attracting parents and prospective pupils to the school.

Where schools support families with additional services by working closely with the local healthcare and social services, many note earlier resolution of family problems and less need for crisis management.

Working with parents/carers of anxious children

Parents of anxious children are often anxious themselves and feel guilty about their child's difficulties. They may find it difficult to talk to staff about their child's difficulties, feeling that it will reflect badly on them or that their child will not be given the same respect as other children. Parents want staff to care about their children as individuals and to have the same high expectations for all of them. Ways of engaging parents who have anxious children should be explored specifically. Groups run for parents who are concerned about their children's anxiety have been found by the authors to be highly effective. They can help in resolving parents' unease and provide appropriate strategies that can be consistently implemented at home and at school. They offer an opportunity to provide information, encourage the use of new strategies and provide emotional support through the parent network. Further information on running parent workshops can be found in Appendix 4. Resources and advice have been provided with this book to enable staff and parents to work together, develop their knowledge and skills and build trust between home and school.

Working with other professionals

School staff often tell us that they feel a lack of services to help them with needy and vulnerable children. Waiting lists for children and adolescent mental health services (CAMHs) are often long and thresholds are high. Whilst this book aims to assist school staff in working with anxious children and their parents, there will be times when this level of expertise is insufficient. At these points, referrals will need to be made to the appropriate professionals, either directly or by asking parents to request services themselves. This may be the family GP, the social worker, or CAMHs. Educational psychologists may also be able to offer consultations, advice and support. Many schools now employ family liaison officers who can be invaluable in advising parents and helping to build the links between school, family and other professionals. Building trusting relationships with professionals outside the school will pay dividends when the need for assistance arises.

Working with the wider community

Schools play a central role in their community, and those within and outside the school can benefit from working together. Evidence shows that after-school activities can have a positive effect on attainment, behaviour and attendance. According to the 'Narrowing the Gap' document (Waldman, 2008), schools that engaged the entire community in learning had a

> 'direct impact on pupils' attainment and raised their aspirations and determination to progress from school to further education, training or employment'.

Increasing the range of situations in which children learn and the number of people that they can learn with enriches their curriculum and extends their skills.

Support from parents and local community organisations can be crucial in combating social exclusion and in improving pupils' attainment, motivation and expectations. Schools in the most disadvantaged communities can play a vital role in providing access to core services that are often not available locally and which are essential for helping address health inequalities, poverty and social exclusion – sometimes simply by use of school premises.

Participation in consultation and decision-making processes will strengthen the relationship between children, young people and the school/community. This has been shown to increase young people's pride and engagement with their local communities, improve community spirit and reduce crime in the area.

The reputation of a school may be enhanced through its pupils' involvement in community projects.

Conclusion

There are a number of whole-school practices which can help to address the difficulties faced by children and young people showing anxiety and make it more likely that they will thrive academically, socially and emotionally. These are effective leadership, values and aims underpinning policies that are owned by the school community, careful attention to the pastoral care system, a good curriculum and physical environment, plus close working with parents/carers and the wider community. These will benefit not only anxious children but the whole school community.

Summary

Leadership, values and aims

➤ Effective schools
➤ Ethos and values
➤ The importance of policies

Systems and practices

➤ Relationship building and pastoral care
➤ Curriculum
➤ Physical environment

Working with others

➤ Working with parents/carers
➤ Working with parents/carers of anxious children
➤ Working with other professionals
➤ Working with the wider community

Conclusion

5 | Anxiety in the classroom

Introduction

Teachers are a great influence on children and young people and their importance should not be underestimated. Children benefit from adults outside the family 'being available' when life experiences are difficult to manage. Teachers may well become trusted adults who offer an emotionally safe environment in which to express fears and worries when life is challenging. Teachers are not social workers and most do not have a counselling qualification, but the majority of teachers and assistants in primary schools and the pastoral support teachers and assistants in secondary schools have opportunities to provide emotional support for children and young people.

All children experience difficult emotions. Sadness, anxiety and insecurity are all normal and we should not be attempting to eliminate uncomfortable feelings, but rather offer support with strategies to manage them. There is no need to assume automatically that there is a mental health difficulty when anxiety and stress are being experienced; the ups and downs of life are normal. When they are being managed reasonably well, or are transitory and in response to a specific event in the child's life, they are unlikely to constitute a mental health problem:

> 'the notion of a life well lived, including tragedy, suffering, pain, happiness is about being able to experience the fullness of life and still flourish.'
>
> Aristotle

However, if the level of anxiety is preventing children and young people from engaging in learning, it will affect their ability to reach their full potential. We know that anxiety can affect school life significantly in a variety of ways, including academic and social emotional experiences.

Anxiety may present as difficulties in:

- attendance
- asking for help
- speaking-up in class
- mixing with peers
- talking to teachers
- participating in some activities; for example, PE, eating in public, managing large groups of people

40

- learning processes; for example, information processing, memory
- regulation of emotions.

This chapter will consider a number of approaches teachers can consider in order to provide a supportive classroom environment once the wider school systems are in place and being consistently applied (see Chapter 4).

How can I tell if a student has anxiety?

Recognising signs and symptoms

Children do not tend to talk about their anxiety and often they may not know that what they are feeling is called anxiety. Sometimes it can be difficult to differentiate from a bad mood, feeling unwell, pushing at the boundaries and nervousness. Children may hide their anxiety because they do not know how to express it to others. Children may respond to their anxiety by having angry outbursts or defiant behaviour. If this is responded to with disapproval and discipline it may make the child more anxious and turn into a vicious cycle, which perpetuates the behaviours and the distress for both children and adults.

The following checklist can help in recognising the symptoms of anxiety:

- Negative thought patterns, imagining the worst; for example, I have a headache, I think I have a brain tumour and am going to die
- Constant worrying about things that might happen (the future) or things that have happened (the past). Finding it difficult to stay in the present
- Over-exaggerating the negatives; for example, this always happens to me, I never get it right, or I will never be able to go to college, get a job (catastrophising)
- Self-criticism, perfectionism; for example, this isn't good enough, I must do better
- Guilty thoughts and feelings; for example, I should not have said that to . . . I will not have any friends now
- Aggression may be subtle or obvious, as in angry outbursts
- Opposition and defiance
- Inattention and restlessness
- Frequent crying
- Physical complaints; for example, stomach aches, headaches, sickness, tiredness
- Avoidance behaviours: avoiding people, situations, places and refusing to take part in activities
- Sleeping difficulties.

(adapted from Mendability's online Sensory Enrichment Therapy)

Panic attacks

In some cases anxiety is extremely obvious, and this is likely to be the case if a child has a panic attack. A panic attack is a sudden episode of intense fear with severe physical reactions when there is no real danger or apparent cause. A person having a panic attack might think they are losing control, having a heart attack, or even dying. Observers of a panic attack may also be convinced that the very real physical symptoms imply a life-threatening condition, and it is not unusual for emergency services to be called to a person suffering such an attack. The duration can vary from seconds to hours. Panic attacks themselves are not physically dangerous but very frightening for the person concerned and sometimes for those present with them. The subsequent fear of further panic attacks can increase levels of anxiety and encourage avoidance and safety behaviours.

How to help?

If it is possible that this a serious medical event, and not a panic attack, medical help should be summoned.

However, a child or young person who has repeated panic attacks in school may be able to take part with parents and school staff in agreeing a suitable plan, which is likely to include the following elements:

- if possible, move the child/young person to a safe, quiet space where there is no audience of classmates
- stay with them until the panic attack has subsided
- let the panic run its course, as trying to stop it may fuel it
- stay calm and reassuring, speak slowly and calmly
- remind them that they are safe and that this will pass
- encourage them to breathe, concentrating on slowing the breathing down
- physical touch may be reassuring; for example, back stroking, if this agreed with the parent and the child.

After the panic attack has subsided the student may feel embarrassed and upset that it has happened. Reassurance and positive affirmation will be important at this stage. Children quite often become hungry/thirsty or exhausted after a panic attack, so offering a snack/drink and some time to settle or rest before returning to normal class routines will be helpful.

It would be good to encourage the practising of breathing exercises when they are calm as it is easier to learn new skills at this time. If the child/young person can form the habit of deep breathing it will be easier for them to call on this strategy when they are very anxious (see Part 4).

Ensure parents are kept informed and that discussions about appropriate support both in and out of school take place.

Building relationships

Anxious children benefit significantly from developing good relationships with their teachers. If they feel valued and respected it helps them to feel safe and secure. Listening to children effectively is one of the most important skills we can utilise. Within busy family lives it is often difficult to find the time to listen to children and young people and hear what they are feeling. This is also true in a busy classroom. However, being listened to makes us feel worthwhile and special, and will also make it easier for students to feel they can talk to you about their worries and concerns when they are ready to.

> 'At the heart of a positive classroom is the children's knowledge that they will be listened to.'
>
> Jenny Mosley

Sometimes it is difficult to feel that we are making a difference for children, especially those who have challenging home environments, but it should be remembered that simply being someone who children or young people can rely on and trust will make a big difference. All children and young people benefit from this, but those experiencing anxiety difficulties will find it easier to stay relaxed and calm when they are with a person who they know will be there to listen to them when they need some attention.

Quality circle time

Quality circle time is a well-known and highly respected method for helping to develop positive relationships in the classroom (Mosley, 1996). This provides a forum for children to be able to work together with adults to promote social emotional skills. It is an excellent way to build relationships both between adults and children and between the children themselves. The benefits, from the perspective of a pupil with anxiety difficulties, are:

- students are able to help and support each other
- they develop an ability to talk about feelings, worries and concerns
- each child and young person is equally involved, so that the anxious, quiet, child with little confidence and low self-esteem will have the same access to involvement as that for some of the more outgoing and chatty children.

Circle time can provide an ideal forum for developing group listening skills. This offers a practical way to discuss concerns, think about solutions and formulate plans.

Talking and listening

When children are ready to discuss things that are worrying them, and this may not be until you have built up a trusting relationship with them, there are a number of techniques that can be helpful for promoting a useful conversation.

Younger children

Young children do not have the resources for thinking through difficult feelings, they do not talk naturally or easily about their troubling feelings, neither do they talk to each other about their feelings. Things can go wrong using language alone because:

- Feelings are misrepresented by the child; for example, 'I'm bored', 'I'm cross'
- Feelings are denied: 'Nothing's wrong,' 'I'm OK'.

Direct speaking is not the natural language of feelings for children. Their natural language is that of image and metaphor. Using drawings and play can allow children to express themselves in a more effective way. Excellent ideas for drawing are provided by Margot Sunderland in *Draw on Your Emotions* (1997).

Older children and young people

Some young people are comfortable talking individually in a quiet space with an adult, but others find it embarrassing and difficult. For these young people it can help to talk whilst you are doing an activity of some sort. This could be going for a walk as you talk, having the young person help with a simple task, or sharing some age-appropriate colouring or art activity whilst talking. This takes the direct personal pressure off the young person and provides plenty of opportunities for moments of thoughtful silence or talk about less stressful matters as the relationship is being built. The conversation that is not directly about the problem may also give you information about the young person's resources and strategies that you can draw on in advising them. Reducing eye contact and pressure to talk about the problem in this way makes it far less intense and more manageable for those who are less comfortable talking about themselves.

A range of questions has been identified by Natasha Devon (a mental health expert) as being effective in helping children and young people to think about ways to move forward rather than just going around in the same circles.

1. What would you like to happen?
2. OK, what out of that list do you have the power to change?
3. Who can help you with that?
4. How much of your time are you spending thinking about that?

5. What's the worst that can happen?
6. What's the best that can happen?
7. What advice would you give to a friend who came to you with this dilemma?
   (Natasha Devon, MBE, is the former government mental health champion)

Active listening

Listening is the most fundamental component of interpersonal communication.

It sounds like an easy thing to do, but to do it well can be challenging and time consuming. When listening to an individual child/young person it is important to be sure you have understood the messages from the other person. It is easy to jump to conclusions, make assumptions and provide solutions developed from your own perspective. To listen effectively we need to:

- give full attention to the speaker
- not interrupt
- convey interest by giving eye contact, nodding and smiling
- notice the other person's body language; is it consistent with what they are telling you?
- encourage them to continue by using simple prompts; 'yes', 'mmm'
- wait for a pause before speaking
- only ask questions for clarification
- try to understand the issue from the other person's perspective
- try to understand how the other person is feeling
- briefly summarise what you think they are saying.

This may need some practising if you are not familiar with it. Practising with a colleague and getting feedback from them would be helpful. More information on communication with young people can be found in the reference for Nick Luxmoore (2000).

Areas of anxiety commonly seen in mainstream schools

The teacher in a mainstream classroom is likely to meet children and young people with the following types of anxiety.

Maths anxiety

Maths anxiety is becoming increasingly recognised in psychology and education and is a valid phenomenon that can affect people of all abilities.

One definition that the authors have found helpful is that maths anxiety is:

'a debilitating emotional reaction to mathematics.'

(Cambridge University's Centre for Neuroscience in Education)

Most of us who have worked in the classroom will have experienced working with children who 'freeze', or feel ill, in the face of a maths test or learning a new maths concept, despite having the ability to complete the work successfully. Some children may even have difficulty attending school on days with maths on the timetable. However, it may be less obvious when it is manifested in challenging or oppositional behaviours.

Research has shown that the brain activation patterns associated with physical pain can be observed when people who have maths anxiety are exposed just to the thought of a maths problem (Foley et al, 2017).

How to help

It is important for teachers not to say anything blatantly negative about maths; for example, 'I've always found maths difficult', 'Maths is very hard'. Children and young people may also 'learn' the behaviour in their home environment. Parents who found maths difficult at school may inadvertently be reinforcing their child's difficulties, saying 'I'm rubbish at maths', or 'I could never do maths at school'. This can be particularly true when parents are trying to help children with maths homework and find that the methods have changed, leaving them feeling incompetent and unsure of their own abilities. In this way children can feel that being afraid of maths is somehow legitimised and that it is OK to be poor at maths if mum and/or dad are. It is easy for adults to pass on their own anxiety to children and young people.

Staying positive and using positive language when working with children on the maths curriculum will help children who are prone to maths anxiety.

Exam/test anxiety

As we have discussed earlier in the book, normal levels of stress help us to work more efficiently, think faster and improve performance generally. When anxiety becomes overwhelming, however, performance will be affected. This in turn can lead to a cycle of negative expectations being reinforced, more anxiety and negative self-talk in the future getting more extreme. Thus negative beliefs become a self-fulfilling prophesy.

To help children and young people manage their anxiety, the following checklist may be helpful. Help students to:

● develop, in advance, relaxation techniques that work for them, practising the techniques when they are calm

FIGURE 5.1 Cycle of negative beliefs

- lead a healthy lifestyle
- take time to wind down before going to bed
- avoid perfectionism
- plan revision and start revision early
- be realistic about how much can be revised in what timescale
- have a checklist of helpful thoughts, behaviours and relaxation techniques and decide when you will need to use them
- positive affirmations
- reframe difficult physiological feelings as your body preparing to help you work at your best.

Further advice on coping with exam/test anxiety is provided by St. Andrew's University (see Useful websites).

Further details and help in managing emotions, changing unhelpful thoughts, developing healthy behaviours and managing physiological symptoms are available in the Practical Interventions section of this book, in Part 4.

Social anxiety

Students experiencing social anxiety may have difficulty joining in with social situations and worry about what other people think of them. They may become acutely embarrassed when attention is placed on them and be unable to respond in the same way as other students.

Children and young people with social anxiety in the classroom are likely to demonstrate the following behaviours:

- avoiding eye contact
- reluctance to answer questions
- difficulty sharing ideas and work
- physical symptoms; for example, blushing, shaking, stammering, restlessness when attention is drawn to them.

Often children in this situation will 'freeze', affecting memory and information-processing skills. It is important to take the individual pressure off the student at that time and find an alternative way to help them contribute to class discussion and group work. Waiting for them to answer or criticising them for not contributing will make matters worse, not better.

How to help

- Create an atmosphere in which thinking aloud is valued
- Encourage children to start their answers with 'I think . . . '
- Change language from 'what is . . . ?' and 'what does . . . ?' to 'what could . . . ?' and 'what do you think . . . ?' This indicates you are interested in their ideas and thought processes rather than finding the 'correct' answer
- Encourage written ideas, in the classroom notice and praise
- Encourage children to talk to each other before answering questions individually
- Avoid drawing attention to them
- Ask their opinions about a topic privately
- Let them know you are always happy to talk
- Start a peer-to-peer support system.

Separation anxiety

It is normal for a young child to feel anxious about leaving their parents or primary caregivers, but when it persists over time, becomes very intense or begins to interfere with school life then it will need some attention. For normal developmental stages associated with separation anxiety, see Chapter 3.

Working in close collaboration with parents/carers is very important when dealing with separation anxiety. Consistency between home and school will make it easier for the child to feel safe and secure. If it becomes so intense that the child is refusing to come to school or feeling ill to avoid attending, it is important to encourage the child to get back to school as soon as possible. The longer a child is away from school the more difficult it will be for him/her to attend comfortably. Parents themselves may need more support than is typically available from school staff and may benefit from specialist support if the issue is not quickly resolved.

How to help

- Consider the child's programme at school and see if it needs adapting
- Find out if there are any difficulties with other children that need addressing
- Have a highly structured, graduated plan for return to school after a period of absence
- Accommodate late arrival, shorter days if necessary
- Ensure staff in the office are aware of the child's difficulties so that they can praise the child for arriving, even if late
- Reward the child for managing small steps
- Identify a safe place in the school for the child to go to if needed
- Provide someone to 'meet and greet' to help the child get over the initial transition from home to school
- Help parents to stay calm, set firm limits and apply them consistently
- Help parents to develop a goodbye ritual and then leave without fuss
- Provide support with social interactions and transitions
- Consider a buddy system
- Therapeutic stories can help younger children; for example, *The Invisible String* (Karst, 2001) and *I Love You All Day Long* (Rusakas, 2008).

Children can benefit enormously by having appropriate support at the right time in their lives. If a difficulty is addressed early and effectively it will be less likely to develop into a mental health difficulty later in life.

Classroom culture

Routines

Routines provide predictability and security in the classroom and around the school. Being confident about what is expected can significantly reduce levels of anxiety. It also means that teachers have more time for teaching and learning and that low-level behaviour difficulties will be minimised. This in turn will create a calmer working environment for all students. Routines will need to be taught, modelled and practised. This may take the first couple of weeks of the school year. Short reminders will be needed at the beginning of the day/lesson so that routines stay fresh in students' minds.

Decide which times of the day would benefit from clear routines, bearing in mind that transitions are particularly stressful for some students.

The following times of the day/activities could be considered in the first instance:

- Beginning of the day
- Entering and exiting the classroom
- Signalling for quiet and attention
- Handing out books
- Tidying equipment
- Transitioning from one activity to another
- Moving around the school
- End of the day.

Students enjoy being given jobs of responsibility within these routines. These can be rotated around the students. Where feasible it is helpful to pre-warn if a change of routine is necessary, so that students do not become anxious and distressed. Some teachers like to use clear markers for particular routines; for example, specific pieces of music, visual symbols, auditory symbols.

The benefits of clear routines have been seen to be particularly beneficial to students with specific difficulties, such as ADHD and ASC. However, it is also clear that most children benefit from reducing the uncertainty about 'what do I do next' in the classroom and around the school.

The habits and routines we develop as adults help us to do some tasks without thinking about them, such as driving a car. This enables our brains to attend to more intellectually demanding tasks such as memorising new skills, problem solving, analysing, predicting and planning. In the same way, if children know, for instance, where and when to hang their coats, collect their books and sit, this both gives a sense of security and frees their minds for learning.

Positive behaviour management

Anxious students often have poor self-esteem and can be easily distressed by criticism.

Ensuring that the behaviour plan in your class is based on positive rules makes it easier for them to see what they should do, rather than what they shouldn't. This will help in understanding how to behave in the classroom whilst maintaining self-esteem.

Consequences need to be relevant to, and in proportion with, the behaviours. Punishments which depend on invoking fear to encourage compliance will not be helpful to a student who is already prone to anxiety.

Positive encouragement and acknowledgement of success (even tiny successes) should be used at least three times as often as negative comments or reprimands. This will establish a positive atmosphere in which it is safe to receive an occasional reminder of the rules. Anxious students benefit from being given some individual positive encouragement early in the lesson.

Consistency is a very important aspect of classroom management. All children should have equal access to rewards and positive recognition. Anxious children find it difficult to manage uncertainty and will become more unsettled if they cannot be sure how people are going to respond. Behaviour can be viewed as a form of communication and, as such, can give us clues about how the child or young person is feeling and what they are thinking. For instance, a refusal to work may be communicating an anxiety that the student fears they are unable to do the work successfully. Identifying the message within the behaviour can help us to consider teaching alternative, more appropriate, behaviours which give the same message.

Communicating with children and young people

It is important with children and young people that our communication is clear and unambiguous. Our language needs to be assertive and at an appropriate language level for the developmental level of the students. Assertiveness is a communication style in which a person stands up for their own needs and beliefs whilst also respecting the needs of others. An assertive adult states expectations clearly, confidently and consistently and is prepared to back up words with actions. Children and young people learn to trust and respect an assertive adult as they clearly know what is expected of them. For anxious students this is particularly important.

Don't underestimate the power of non-verbal communication. If a spoken message conflicts with body language and/or tone of voice, it is the non-verbal message that tends to be 'heard'. Consider the different ways that you can say *'Yes, that work is good enough!'* as an example of how powerful the non-verbal messages can be. Teachers may choose to try it out with a friend or colleague and then watch out for other mismatches between verbal and non-verbal communication.

Taking account of the way we think, feel and behave is a crucial element in working with anxious students. It is easy to 'pass on' anxiety to others. If we are feeling anxious and unsure of ourselves, children will pick that up (emotional mirroring) and feel less secure and emotionally safe in the classroom. Confidence and trust in ourselves can help to reduce students' anxiety in the classroom.

Growth mindset

The classroom needs to be a safe place to try things out during learning, and, therefore, understanding that getting things 'wrong' is an intrinsic part of learning is very important. The acronym FAIL – First Attempt In Learning – can be useful. Effort does not always equate with success, and it is important to recognise the importance of effort so that students do not get disheartened.

Growth mindset is a theory of learning that was developed by Carol Dweck in the 1990s. She argues that people fall somewhere on the continuum between a fixed mindset and growth mindset. A fixed mindset occurs if the person believes that their success in any area of their life is based on luck or innate abilities, whereas growth mindset is present if it is believed that success can be achieved through hard work, effort and practice. Naturally, if we do not believe we can improve our abilities by working at them our motivation will be lower.

We may not know whether we have a fixed or growth mindset, but it can usually be seen in our response to failure. The person with a fixed mindset will become very distressed by failure as they will think that it reflects on their abilities, about which they can do nothing. With a growth mindset, failure is managed better as there is a belief that future performance can be improved with effort.

Those with growth mindsets have been found to lead less stressful and more successful lives. A fixed mindset, on the other hand, can lead to stress and anxiety. Clearly for a child or young person prone to anxiety it will be helpful to adopt strategies that help them to believe that challenges can be opportunities rather than threats, and that they can change and make improvements over time.

Growth mindset can be encouraged by praising effort, not talent; for example, 'That is a great piece of work, you've worked very hard', rather than 'That is a great piece of work, you are very clever'. Encourage children to say 'I cannot manage this problem yet', rather than 'I cannot manage this problem'.

Curriculum

Some children and young people, even with a supportive classroom environment, need extra support to develop their social emotional skills. Most British schools now have a range of resources available to support students in the classroom, individually and/or in small groups. In some areas, schools are developing the role of the emotional literacy support assistant to work specifically with children and young people with social and emotional difficulties. There are many resources available to support the teaching of social skills, but it is important to structure the interventions to the specific needs of the students involved. As with academic subjects, prerequisite skills will need to be identified and addressed and topics may need to be broken down into small steps. Opportunities for practising and generalising new skills are also crucial aspects of learning.

Social skills

Specific components of an effective curriculum include the following:

- good turn-taking skills
- ability to share appropriately
- ability to follow reasonable directions
- ability to follow rules of play/games/classroom
- joining in groups for tasks and fun
- ignoring provocation and other distractions
- offering praise and compliments
- receiving praise
- managing anger (own and others)
- forming and maintaining successful relationships with peers and adults.

Friendship skills

Some children and young people are naturally good at forming and maintaining friendships, others find it more difficult and may need help to learn the skills. The following aspects may be helpful for some children. Learn how to:

- understand what a friend is
- appreciate your own strengths
- appreciate others' strengths
- use polite and kind words
- listen and show you care
- give compliments
- take turns and share
- celebrate others' successes
- try new activities with others
- offer to help others
- solve conflicts peacefully
- understand about others' feelings.

Teaching children and young people communication skills

Effective communication can have a significant impact on relationships and managing the social world. Some of the elements staff might want to consider include:

- good listening skills
- taking turns in conversation

- good speaking skills (rate, tone, volume)
- expressing views, feelings and ideas appropriately
- seeking help appropriately
- understanding and using effective body language.

Each of the skills above are open to creative teaching methods such as drama, role play, journalism, community service, games, outward-bound activities and sport. It is often better to help children manage these underlying basic social emotional skills before addressing the anxiety directly.

Building resilience

It is important that we support children and young people in developing long-term coping strategies to help them manage and bounce back from difficulties that we cannot change or control.

Growth mindset, as discussed in the previous section, is one aspect of building resilience. Others include:

- developing a sense of self and self-worth
- developing confidence and competence
- problem solving
- developing interests and out-of-school activities
- learning about taking personal responsibility and fulfilling obligations to others
- having a sense of belonging in school
- having good relationships with family and friends
- understanding and managing emotions, both their own and others
- understanding boundaries and keeping within them.

There are many ways to support children and young people in developing these skills.

Further support for developing resilience can be found in the *Mental Health and Resilience Therapy Toolkit* (Hart and Taylor, 2011).

Should you feel that you need to address anxiety directly with several children in your class, you can find resources to help you run classroom and/or group sessions on anxiety in Chapter 9.

Conclusion

The explanations and strategies provided above will help in understanding and supporting the majority of children and young people within a mainstream classroom.

More severe anxiety may require specialist assistance. If classroom teachers feel that further support is needed, they should talk to their special educational needs coordinator in the first instance. It may be that further outside support will be considered appropriate.

Summary

Introduction

How can I tell if a student has anxiety?

➤ Recognising signs and symptoms
➤ Panic attacks

Building relationships

➤ Quality circle time
➤ Talking and listening

Areas of anxiety commonly seen in mainstream schools

➤ Maths anxiety
➤ Exam/test anxiety
➤ Social anxiety
➤ Separation anxiety

Classroom culture

➤ Routines
➤ Positive behaviour management
➤ Communicating with children and young people
➤ Growth mindset

Curriculum

➤ Social skills
➤ Friendship skills
➤ Teaching children and young people communication skills
➤ Building resilience

Conclusion

6 | Preparing to work with small groups and/or individuals

Introduction

Intervening early when children and young people are experiencing anxiety is important in helping to avoid mental health problems occurring later in life. The limits on availability and of speed of access to specialist mental health services mean that parents/carers and professionals working with children need to have the confidence and the tools to provide support in a safe and structured way. This chapter provides guidance on how to work with groups of children, individual children and young people (see Chapters 9 and 10 for detailed plans). It is important to stress, however, that when engaging in this kind of work staff should only take on what they feel comfortable doing and that they should get support whenever needed. These interventions do not replace the need for specialist mental health support, but may provide ways to intervene in mild anxiety, the early stages of anxiety and/or whilst waiting for specialist help.

In order to decide the type of support a child/young person would benefit from, please read Chapter 3 to establish whether the fears that are being experienced are within the normal range. It may be that the anxiety is within the normal range for the age of the child/young person and that it will dissipate as the individual matures. This is not to say that there is nothing that can be done, and Chapter 3 provides many suggestions on how to provide support at each stage. Non-intrusive forms of support can be offered and most children will benefit from learning about anxiety and how to manage it.

It is also important to ensure that the environment within which the children/young people are experiencing anxiety – schools and classrooms, for example – are organised in ways that reduce the probability of anxiety either before intervening or alongside the interventions (see Chapters 4 and 5).

General issues

Informed consent

Whenever school staff provide individual or small-group work for children and young people which is related to mental health issues, it is advisable to gain informed consent from parents/carers and the children themselves. If support takes the form of building resilience, as might be the case for a whole-class intervention, it may be more appropriate simply to inform parents. Other professionals will have their own arrangements for informed consent.

Parents/carers

For professionals working with individuals or small groups of children, it is good practice to discuss the expectations with parents/carers before the work begins. Some parents/carers may have expectations which do not fit with the model presented, others may reflect a lack of understanding of the importance of emotional safety and security for the child/young person. Reaching a clear understanding prior to starting the work is an important part of obtaining informed consent from parents/carers. For instance, expecting to eradicate anxiety completely could be unhelpful when working with anxious children. We all feel anxious at times and this is a healthy reaction (see Chapter 1). The aim of these interventions is to help to manage the anxiety so that it improves the quality of everyday life.

Children/young people

For small-group or individual work which is optional, it is good practice to allow children and young people a preparatory session so they can gain an understanding of the nature of the sessions that will be provided for them. They will then be able to consider whether they would like to be involved. If it is felt that a child/young person has such a significant need that they urgently require support, it is sensible to refer to the GP and/or mental health specialists.

It may be that some children/young people would be more suited to individual work whilst others would benefit from the support of their peers in a group setting. This will depend on the severity of the symptoms and the personality of the child/young person. For group work, the make-up of the group will need careful consideration and management (see 'Working with groups' below).

The group-work sessions provided in Chapter 9 can be easily adapted for whole-class work, in which case there will be less exploration of children's personal experiences and a greater emphasis on giving information. In this case, children might not be given the opportunity to opt out. If this path is taken it is good practice to inform the parents of all children taking part.

Parents working with their own children

Chapter 7 considers the home specifically and offers advice suitable to that situation. However, this should not prevent parents using activities and worksheets provided in

Part 4 if they feel comfortable doing so. Parents will know their own children best and may pick and choose the most relevant activities.

Motivation for change

Parents who consider anxiety to be adversely affecting academic learning, social interactions and/or family life may well request help from school staff. However, it is important to consider how motivated the child/young person is to change and whether their perception of the issues is the same as the parents'. Who is the problem owner, the child/young person or the parent? Equally, if the teacher is the one who is concerned, the teacher could be considered the 'problem owner' if parents and/or the child are less concerned. Whilst it is the child that will receive the intervention, he or she may not be motivated to change. There are some forms of anxiety – separation anxiety, for example – which need a family-based approach to support change. Working with an individual alone may not change the dynamics which have resulted in, and are maintaining, the anxiety.

It is extremely difficult to effect change with an individual who is unwilling or lacks motivation to change. It may not be the right time to involve the student in group or individual sessions if they are not interested in working on their anxiety.

Within motivational interviewing (see Chapter 1 for further explanation of this approach), there is a model which helps us to understand the individual's readiness for making behavioural change (Prochaska and DiClemente, 1983). The 'Stages of change' diagram below illustrates the phases of this model (precontemplation, contemplation, preparation, action, maintenance, relapse).

It is important that we recognise where the child/young person is in this cycle so that we can help them move on to the next stage.

Our behaviours develop as strategies for getting our needs met, albeit inappropriately at times. It is possible, therefore, that a child is getting 'secondary gains' from the anxious behaviours. These are sometimes known as 'payoffs'. The four most typical 'payoffs' for inappropriate anxiety behaviours are:

- we get to feel good
- we get to avoid or get rid of uncomfortable thoughts and feelings
- we get to escape from an unpleasant situation
- we get attention.

(Taken from Harris, 2013)

For example, one of our clients, a ten-year-old girl, stated openly that she had no wish to get over her anxiety of being separated from her mother. This was because, as a result

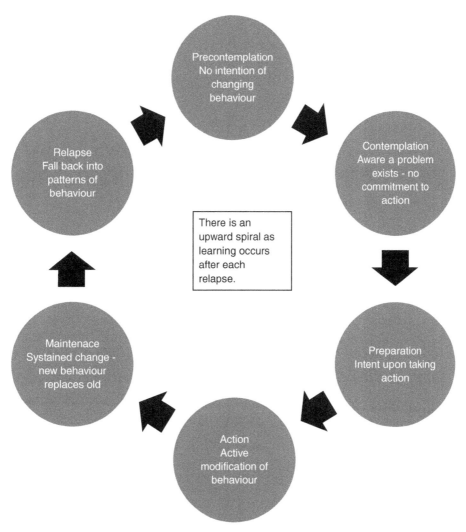

FIGURE 6.1 Stages of change
www.psychologytools.com

of being too anxious to be separated from her mother, she was taken by her mother on business trips which were 'really fun' and much better than staying at home with her dad and going to school. Typically, such payoffs are less obvious and usually not discussed openly. Parents, too, may be receiving 'payoffs' from their child's anxiety. This could be as simple as the pleasure of feeling especially loved and needed by the anxious child.

It is important to realise that this can be inadvertently reinforced by adults as well as young people or children themselves. Awareness of these issues will be important in working towards successful outcomes with children and young people.

Supervision

Professionals

There are many types of supervision that may be available for professionals working with children and young people. The two types that are important for this work are professional supervision and clinical supervision. These two types of supervision would normally be provided separately.

Professional supervision is a performance-related, managerial role. It involves working closely with the professional team/network to ensure that the work you are planning fits with the ethos, aims and objectives of the wider institution within which the work is being promoted. This will include reference to individual performance targets and general ongoing support as the work proceeds.

Clinical supervision involves addressing the emotional needs of the supervisee. It is a formal, collaborative process taken on by those with the skills of supervision. The purpose of clinical supervision is to help the supervisee learn from his or her experience and to understand any personal agendas or issues which may be affecting the work in progress. It also provides a form of quality control and ensures safe practice for both the supervisee and the client.

The type of supervision provided/sought will depend on the nature of the work and the skills of the supervisee. It is likely, for example, that those working with groups and individuals at the level of developing anxiety management tools would receive professional supervision only. However, those working with individuals may benefit from receiving clinical supervision. It is important that all practitioners work in line with their own professional code of ethics and conduct.

It is not within the scope of this book to provide more details about supervision, but to raise awareness that these issues must be considered whenever adults are working with children with mental health issues.

Parents

Although it would not be expected that parents working with their own children would need supervision, it is recommended that support groups are joined. Some schools are beginning to run parent workshops and small-group support for those with anxious children. Resources for parent groups can be found in Appendix 4. There are also support networks online and in community localities. Young Minds is a good starting point when looking for support from professionals and other parents (see Useful websites).

Additional resources and support can be found at anxiety.co.uk, the national charity's website. Further information concerning different types of supervision can be found at the British Association for Counselling and Psychotherapy (BACP). There is also an e-learning facility which can be found at the London Deanery (see Useful websites).

Working with small groups

Process

Working with children/young people in a group, rather than individually, can have benefits both for the children/young people and for the efficient use of time and resources.

It will involve a structured and directed approach, with specific issues being covered in each session. However, to some extent a child-centred approach can be adopted within this framework through discussion, to allow children and young people to explore and resolve the thoughts and feelings they have. Change must take place within the individual if it is to be effective and sustainable. The aim is to bridge the gap between wanting to change and the reality of trying out new ways of managing feelings, thoughts and behaviours, which can feel very daunting and scary. When working in a group there are fewer opportunities to follow each student's personal journey than is the case with individual work, but work can still be tailored to some extent with a small group.

Working in a group allows children to learn from one another, recognise that other children also experience anxiety, possibly about different things. Students can learn to support each other both within the group and in the wider environment. As well as learning from the formal content of the sessions, the incidental learning that takes place in group work can be very valuable. Group work is an ideal setting in which to help students understand the effect their behaviour has on others; for example, interrupting, not taking turns, not engaging. This helps with understanding social interactions and how alternative perspectives can lead to misunderstandings which may increase anxiety. It is helpful for the group facilitator to be able to discuss the behaviours within the group in a non-judgemental way so that children feel safe to explore alternative ideas and feelings.

Ground rules

In order to create a safe environment it is important to set some ground rules. These can be negotiated with the students in the introductory session and could include:

- respect one another and avoid negative or judgemental comments
- take turns
- listen when someone else is speaking
- try to take part in activities but use the 'right to pass' if you feel uncomfortable.

Children/young people may decide on some rules of their own which are specific to the setting. This is fine if all the participants agree and they are manageable for all the group members. There should not be more than about four or five rules, depending on the age of the children/young people. The ground rules should be rehearsed at the beginning of each session and reinforced positively by the group facilitator and co-worker, if there is one.

Choosing the group

The optimum size of group for this type of intervention is three to five pupils of similar age and with similar issues.

When considering who will participate in a group for children/young people experiencing anxiety, remember to consider the dynamics among students. It is particularly important, when working with such a sensitive issue as anxiety, that the students feel emotionally 'safe' within the group and the participants should be chosen accordingly. For example, siblings might not feel comfortable expressing themselves freely in front of each other and it may be necessary to consider any community issues or previously existing relationships that are of current concern. It is advised that students attend on a voluntary basis, as motivation and desire to change are important in making life changes. Motivation can be affected by many things, including parental attitude and any 'payoffs' from the anxiety. Belonging to a group such as this may enhance motivation, as students see others overcoming their issues. Anxiety is often closely related to depression, which reduces energy and therefore motivation to change. If a child's depression is such that they cannot access a group intervention, referral to the specialist mental health provider, usually through the GP, should be considered.

Prerequisite skills

Adults

To ensure the emotional safety and well-being of all involved, adults running groups should have prior knowledge and experience of group work and an aptitude for emotionally sensitive work. It may be possible to have a less-experienced adult working alongside an experienced one, to become familiar with the work.

Children/young people

It is important to be aware of the prerequisite skills a child or young person will need to benefit from a group intervention. A child with a social phobia, for example, may benefit more from individual work, at least in the first instance. The developmental levels of the children will need to be understood in order that tasks are appropriately matched to ability levels.

Initial planning

When the group has been chosen it is strongly advised that informed consent is gained from parents and, if appropriate, the students themselves. Ideally this should be discussed with parents and children or young people individually so that they can ask questions safely and do not suffer from peer pressure to attend or not. They then have the choice of whether to join the group. Baseline measures (see below) can be taken at this point.

An initial planning meeting may be run prior to the beginning of the intervention. This should include staff involved in the group directly and those staff who work with the children closely outside the group. If more than one adult will be present at the group it should be agreed in advance who will be the facilitator and who will assist. Clarity about the different functions of these roles should be clear. If time allows, it may be helpful for the group facilitator (or co-worker if there is one) to meet each child between sessions to give support and encouragement particularly related to tasks set. Staff who are not involved directly in the group should be informed that the children's behaviour may change. They may become more open about their feelings at school, when previously they had masked them. This can make it appear that the group work is making the student 'worse' but is, in reality, a reflection of change. It is not unusual for children/young people to mask their feelings at school. They may bottle up their feelings and then become distressed and upset at home as their feelings erupt in the safety of their home environment. This can also be very tiring for the student concerned and lead parents to feel their children are very distressed, whilst school staff may think the child is doing well. It is important that parents feel they can talk to staff about difficulties at home so that these concerns can be addressed as early as possible.

A venue should be chosen which is relatively quiet and private and provides the necessary resources to enable the smooth running of the group; for example, internet access, a flipchart, tables, pens, pencils, water etc. Interruptions or changing venue half way through a session is not advisable. Where possible, it is beneficial to stick to the same venue for each session so that the students feel comfortable and secure and can predict where they will be in the next session.

Difficulties arising during the intervention

The progress of the group should be monitored closely and discussed by the group facilitator and co-worker. If there is a single adult leading the work it is important that this adult has access to supervision (see above). This is sensitive work and the needs of the children remain paramount at all times. Their response to the intervention should be carefully monitored. Should it be considered at any point that the intervention is no longer appropriate for a child, changes must be made to meet that child's needs in another way.

Evaluation

Ideally, baseline measures should be taken to establish current behaviours and the level of individual difficulties. Student, parent and staff perspectives on the nature of the problem should be sought prior to the beginning of the sessions. Baseline measures may be as simple as asking parents, teachers and/or the child him/herself to list issues and give a number between one and ten of how great each problem is. Group facilitators may want to develop their own methods of attaining baseline data which relates to specific circumstances.

Alternatively, there are free questionnaires available on the internet, such as the 'Strengths and difficulties questionnaire' (Goodman, 1997), which would be suitable. The authors use the 'Revised children's anxiety and depression scale (RCAD)' (Chorpita et al, 2000) prior to working with children and young people to gain a better understanding of the level and nature of anxiety and to highlight underlying mental health issues that should be considered. However, this may be too detailed and time consuming for some practitioners. Whatever baseline measure is taken, the same one should be administered again after the sessions have finished to assess change. The assessment may be repeated after further time has passed as it is sustained change over time and the ability to generalise new skills into a range of settings which will make the difference to the quality of life.

Group work for other difficulties

The process for running small groups outlined above works equally well for other forms of support; friendship skills, anger management and social skills, for example. Anxiety and anger are often closely related and further information on running anger management groups in school can be found in 'Promoting emotional literacy: anger management groups' (Sharp and Herrick, 2000). *Anger Management: A Practical Guide For Teachers* (Faupel et al, 2017) may also be a helpful resource for those working with anxious/angry children.

Working with individual children and young people

Approach

Individual work requires more knowledge and expertise than group work as the judgement of the adult is constantly called upon. It allows a more flexible approach than when working with groups, where a previously designed framework is helpful. The same theories apply but the individual work will follow the needs of the child or young person and may not therefore address all areas covered in the group work. Non-judgemental, active listening and valuing the autonomy of the child/young person are important in our approach, and the quality of the relationship is paramount. The decision to change is a personal 'choice' and the child/young person needs to be allowed to go at their own pace. The individuals need to be in control of how deeply they delve into their feelings and thoughts to be sure they are ready for each stage of change. The direction of support and pace of work should remain comfortable and safe as the adult responds to the current needs and preferences of the young person. If children have been through troubled times, it is important not to cause distress by talking about the troubles in detail until the child is ready to.

Relaxation and mindfulness techniques have been included in the resources in this book, but it is important to note that:

> 'If a child is suffering abuse at home, being given space and time for thoughts to drift through your head isn't necessarily good.'
>
> Pooky Knightsmith, vice-chair,
> Young People's Mental Health Coalition

Confidentiality

When working with individuals it is essential to be clear about confidentiality before you start. Adults should not offer confidentiality beyond the bounds they can keep. Children need to know that any sensitive information they share about their thoughts and feelings will not be gossiped about, but that information may be shared to help and support them. It is often agreed that the content of the sessions remains confidential unless:

> The client gives permission for information to be shared, and/or the client reveals something which could be endangering themselves or others.

This will need to be discussed with parents and teachers as well as the children prior to beginning the work. Individual arrangements can be agreed, depending on the age of the student and the nature of the difficulties, if this falls in line with the adult's duty of care (DfE, 2017) and professional code of ethics/practice.

If a professional is planning individual work with a child it is advised that he or she meet the parent (and, if appropriate to the child/young person's developmental level, also with them). In this meeting the expectations of the intervention and the motivation to change can be explored. It is also important to establish whether there are any complicating medical, mental health and/or family circumstances, as well as the level of difficulty being described. This may be a good time to take baseline measures (see above). If a professional thinks that the situation warrants more expertise or support than can be offered, referral should be made to professionals with a higher level of expertise.

Now is the time to discuss the expected number and length of sessions. Typically, one might offer six weekly sessions in the first instance and then negotiate whether further work would be helpful. Reliability and regularity are important to the relationship. It is difficult for a young child to give meaningful informed consent, so it can be helpful for the child to have an initial session to find out what it will be like and then be given the option of more meetings. When possible, sticking to an agreed day, time and venue is useful as predictability helps children and young people to feel secure.

Planning for ending the sessions

When working in a small group, or individually with a child/young person, strong relationships can be built up and, if effective, the young people will feel supported. This is one reason that a provisional number of sessions be agreed in advance. Care needs to be taken to remind the children/young people as the sessions continue of how many there are to go. It may be appropriate to arrange one or more follow-up sessions after a set period of time, and/or to arrange brief 'check-ins' to see how the young person is managing after the sessions end. Certificates, group photographs and written compliments from group members may be considered to help end the sessions positively.

Each session also needs its own ending so that the group facilitator can be sure a child/young person is leaving the session on a positive note and not feeling distressed. It is advisable to have a contingency plan for the possibility that a student is unexpectedly distressed in a session that may have brought up strong emotions. This plan may be as simple as allowing the student some time and space with a trusted adult before returning to the busy classroom. It is important to stick to the plan; a group facilitator can easily become over-involved with the children and wish for the sessions to continue to satisfy their own needs. Children and young people may also wish to continue the sessions as they feel safe and secure, rather than generalise their new skills into the wider environment. This, however, is a vital part of the learning process and it is important not to create dependency relationships.

When working with children and young people it is important to remember that anxiety is not an illness that needs to be cured. It is an emotion that we can help to manage effectively.

Summary

General issues

➤ Informed consent
➤ Motivation
➤ Supervision

Working with small groups

➤ Process
➤ Ground rules
➤ Choosing the group
➤ Prerequisite skills
➤ Initial planning
➤ Difficulties arising
➤ Evaluation

Working with individuals

➤ Approach
➤ Confidentiality
➤ Planning for endings

Part 3
Managing anxiety at home

Support and advice for parents/carers

Introduction

This chapter is for parents who are raising a child who is experiencing anxiety and for professionals who are supporting parents. It includes ideas and strategies that can be used by parents at home. In addition to the suggestions in the chapter, parents may wish to use the more detailed strategies outlined in Part 4.

Living and sharing a home with an anxious child or young person can be extremely exhausting, frustrating and worrying. It can make some parents feel like they are failing, that they should be able to control their child's anxiety, that it must be their fault, that they must be doing something wrong, or that they are incompetent. The stress that it can cause to the adults and other children in the family can cause relationship difficulties, ill health and/or difficulties at work. Some find it difficult to understand why their child is anxious and this may lead to worried hours going over what has happened to them to make them like this. In fact, anxiety is caused by a complex interaction of environmental and individual factors. Anxiety does run in families, there is a known genetic element, just as with the colour of hair or diabetes. That means there is probably someone else in the family who is prone to anxiety, although it may be manifested in different ways. The things that happen to us can also impact on our propensity to suffer from anxiety; trauma, bereavement and family difficulties, for example. However, other children and young people may experience the same issues and not suffer from anxiety-related difficulties. It is possible that we learn some of the characteristics of anxiety from others in the family, although, again, there may be children in the family exposed to the same environment who have learnt different strategies along the way. In this chapter we will explain what anxiety is and what it does to us, as well as looking at how to help our children and how we ourselves can manage anxiety more effectively.

Advice for parents

Anxiety does not have to be caused by trauma or negative experiences and there are several myths that we should consider before we go any further.

Myth One

You should be able to control your child's anxiety

No, you are there to support and guide your child, not try to control their emotions.

Myth Two

Children must change their negative emotions

No, instead children must change their relationship with their negative emotions.

Myth Three

Your child should be anxiety-free

No, anxiety is normal and we need it to keep us safe. Your child needs help to learn to manage anxiety so that it does not interfere with everyday life.

(Adapted from Renee Jain, at www.gozen.com)

How to help

When a child is anxious we are often keen to get rid of the unpleasantness this brings for the child and ourselves. We can say things that are meant to help, but usually don't. When the child is in the middle of an anxiety episode it is not the time to discuss the problem.

Try not to say:
- it is going to be OK, trust me
- there's nothing to be scared of
- let me tell you all the reasons you don't have to worry
- stop being such a worrier
- I don't understand why you are so worried
- don't be silly/childish
- you are spoiling our day out
- you are old enough to manage this now.

Try to be a good role model and keep yourself emotionally healthy. Wait until you and your child are calm before discussing what the anxiety is about and devise a plan together. You may choose to create and use an 'emergency tool kit' for difficult times (see Parts 4 and 5). It may help for you and your child to identify the early signs of anxiety so you can manage the situation before it gets too hard.

Try saying:
- I can see you are very worried about this (acknowledge the feelings)
- I know it feels really bad now, but these feelings will pass

- I am here for you
- try to be brave
- recognise that your child has strengths that will help them – refer to other things they've managed; for example, 'Do you remember how nervous you were doing that swimming competition, and how proud you were afterwards?'

(See '49 phrases to calm an anxious child', at www.gozen.com)

Remember, you have the resources to help and your child has the resources to change. They are still young and learning fast; you can help them to learn effective strategies to manage their difficult feelings.

Separation anxiety

Separation anxiety is an example of anxiety which occurs when children are quite young. Handled appropriately it can lead to children developing resilience and skills to help them in later life.

It is normal for a young child to feel anxious when parents or carers say goodbye; it is a typical stage of development (see Chapter 3). However, if it persists over time, becomes very intense, or begins to interfere with school life then it will need some attention.

If your child is having difficulties separating from you at school it will be important to work closely with the school to devise a plan and agree on appropriate strategies for supporting your child. Consistency between home and school will make it easier for the child to feel safe and secure. If it becomes so intense that the child is refusing to come to school or feeling ill to avoid attending, it is important to encourage the child to get back to school as soon as possible. The longer a child is away from school the more difficult it will be for them to attend comfortably.

There is a lot that parents and teachers can do to help make the child feel safer.

How to help

- Stay patient and calm
- Set firm limits and apply them consistently
- Develop a clear routine for the morning prior to coming to school and keep it consistent
- Develop a goodbye ritual, which may include taking a cuddly toy from home or something of yours that is comforting. This will remind your child of you and of home and provide reassurance that you are coming back to collect them.

Managing anxiety at home

- Offer two appropriate choices, so that your child has some level of control; for example, 'Would you like one hug and two kisses before I leave you at school today, or two hugs and one kiss?', or 'Would you like to keep my scarf with you at school today or your teddy from home?'
- Leave without fuss. Tell your child you are leaving and that you will be back and then leave without hesitating or stalling
- Find out if there is an adult or a 'buddy' your child can stay with when they get to school
- Try not to give in. Make sure you have a support network or a distraction to help you recover from any distress
- Praise your child for any small improvements
- Make sure you have special individual time at home together at the end of the day.

Panic attacks

If the physical symptoms of anxiety become very intense this can lead to panic attacks. A panic attack is when the anxiety becomes so intense that the child/young person is unable to do anything until it subsides. It is difficult to control and it may appear to have come out of nowhere. Your child will be experiencing extreme physical reactions when there is no real danger or apparent cause. When you are having a panic attack you are likely to think that you are losing control, having a heart attack, or even dying. Watching a panic attack can also make you think that the very real physical symptoms are life-threatening. It is not unusual for emergency services to be called to a person suffering a panic attack. The duration can vary from seconds to hours. Panic attacks themselves are not physically dangerous, but very frightening for the person concerned and sometimes for those present with them. The subsequent fear of further panic attacks can increase levels of anxiety and encourage avoidance and safety behaviours.

How to help

If it is possible that this is a serious medical event and not a panic attack, medical help should be summoned. However, panic attacks are not dangerous although they can be frightening. A child who has repeated panic attacks may be able to take part with parents (and, if appropriate, school staff) in agreeing a suitable plan which is likely to include the following elements:

Do
- if possible, take your child somewhere quiet
- stay with them until the panic attack has subsided
- let the panic run its course, as trying to stop it may fuel it

- stay calm and reassuring, speak slowly and calmly
- remind the child that he or she is safe and that this will pass
- encourage the child to breathe, concentrating on slowing the breathing down
- hold, cuddle or stroke your child
- return to normal activities once your child is calm and, if needed, rested.

Do not

- tell the child to calm down
- get cross with your child, or say he or she is naughty, difficult, just being a nuisance
- tell the child to grow up
- tell the child there is nothing to worry about
- try to discuss what the problem is.

After the panic attack has subsided the child may be upset that it has happened. Reassure your child that they are safe and that, although the experience was frightening, they are all right. Physical comfort is likely to be best at this stage. Offer a drink or snack as hunger and thirst often follow panic attacks. Your child may fall asleep soon after a panic attack as it is quite exhausting. If so, allow them to sleep if this is possible. Once the child's physical needs have been taken care of, return to normal activities.

It is helpful to encourage the practise of breathing exercises when your child is calm as it is easier to learn new skills at this time. If children can form the habit of deep breathing it will be easier for them to call on this strategy when they are very anxious (see Parts 4 and 5).

Make sure you discuss your concerns with your child's school, so that you can both provide consistent support for him or her. Appropriate support both in and out of school needs to be planned collaboratively between school staff and parents/carers.

Interventions

The anxiety process

Anxious children are often creative and intelligent, and their sensitivities can be powerful strengths when channelled effectively. If you are reading this chapter your child may have got into the 'habit' of being anxious over several years. If so, learning to manage to control anxiety may take some time and lots of practice. Undoing 'habits' may feel rather frightening as your child may have got used to their anxiety being there with them. Sometimes it is easier to stay with familiar patterns of behaviour even when they make us uncomfortable in the long run. Think of your own efforts to change behaviours; for example, eating, drinking and exercise. It takes time, energy, motivation and plenty of support to change behaviours.

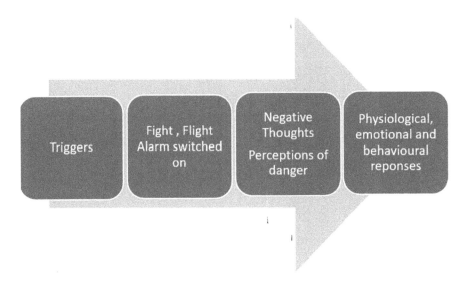

FIGURE 7.1 The anxiety process

When we suffer from anxiety difficulties or disorders our 'emotional alarm' goes off too quickly to a perceived threat rather than a real threat. A good analogy is the smoke alarm going off at home when you are frying bacon. It is reacting to a higher level of danger than is present, although it does alert you to be careful and consider/appraise the situation, which is clearly useful. Children experiencing anxiety are often 'alarmed' by situations when it is not necessary.

Children and young people experiencing high levels of anxiety are more likely to perceive a situation as dangerous when, to others, the same situation will be perceived as exciting or fun or not considered a 'situation' at all. The process of an anxious response involves one or more triggers. An example is going to bed. A negative appraisal of the situation – there could be monsters under my bed – turns on the fight/flight response, leading to a high level of alert to danger. This in turn leads to difficult physical and emotional feelings, more negative thoughts ('I am unwell') and behaviours (I do not go to bed alone), which can be life restricting and reinforcing.

How to help

Helping to manage anxiety involves the following steps:

- Identifying the triggers
- Identifying early signs and signals and providing calming strategies
- Reducing the effects of the fight/flight response
- Managing the emotional responses
- Challenging negative thoughts
- Devising a plan to support facing the fears
- Developing an 'emergency tool box' or 'emotional first aid kit' for difficult situations.

Identifying triggers

When we feel anxious we are responding to a trigger of some sort. These can include:

People (laughing at me, won't like me, making me feel stupid, bullying, ignoring me, not playing with me etc).

Places (school, play parks, swimming pools, crowded places etc).

Situations (changing for PE, firework displays, changes in routine etc).

Animals (insects, dogs, snakes, spiders etc).

Physical feelings (sickness, dizziness, going red, muscle memories from previous situations, trauma etc).

Emotional memories (fear of feeling anxious, emotional memories from a previous situation such as being teased, bullied, ignored, misunderstood etc).

Some children find it hard to talk about what they are worried about. Most children do not know 'why' they are worried. It is difficult to talk about worries and concerns rationally when you are really anxious due to the physical changes in the brain discussed earlier. It is important, therefore, to find a time when you are both calm and there are no potential distractions.

Children may find it difficult to acknowledge or even recognise that they are worried or anxious, so matching your questions to their level of understanding will be important. Keep questions as open as possible; those that cannot be given a Yes/No answer. In this way we encourage our children to open up to their thoughts and not to shut down too quickly from the conversation. We need to be careful not to comment on whether it is right or wrong to be anxious, but to explore the situation openly so that your child can sense that you are hearing his/her point of view and wanting to help.

Questions that may help

What is frightening/worrying/upsetting you?
What do you think will happen when you . . .?
What is it about . . . that is making you feel like this?
What would help you to feel better?
When do you think you will feel better?
What would you say to a friend who was feeling like this?

For children who find it difficult to talk about themselves and their feelings it may be easier for them to write them down or draw them. Sometimes children and young people feel pressured by direct questions. It may be easier for your child/young person to talk about concerns when you are doing things together – cooking or walking, for example – as this takes the pressure off and gives the child more control about the pace and intensity of the discussion.

Identifying early signs and signals

Once someone has reached the peak of their distress it may be harder to alleviate the symptoms than if you notice and intervene early in the anxiety cycle.

You may recognise the early signs of distress. It can be tempting to ignore these and hope they go away. However, this does not usually help. It is more helpful to offer support earlier as it easier for a child to return to calm early on in the emotional anxiety cycle. Parents will often say 'I knew just from the look on his face that this was going to happen'. If that is the case, it is important to identify a number of strategies that might help to restore calm before the distress escalates into a major problem.

Self-soothing/calming strategies

Go outside
Take some exercise
Be creative – drawing, writing, making a model
Listen to music
Use relaxation strategies
Pay attention to all the five senses
Talk about it in a calm environment
Find positive distractions
Drink water

Imagine you are in a safe place; for example, a bedroom, country walk, beach, being with a special friend.

See Parts 4 and 5 for more details on these strategies.

Screen time, although it appears to be a good distraction, increases arousal rather than calms children so do not be tempted to use this as a calming activity. It is more helpful to use it as an incentive/reward for using/managing the calming strategies. See Chapter 8 for more information about managing screen time.

It is best to choose two or three strategies to practise when everyone is calm so that they can become automatic responses when anxiety begins. You may initially need to use rewards to reinforce your child in practising the chosen strategies at calm times, when the child may not see the need. You may need to explain that only when the child is regularly practising the strategies will he/she be able to use them under stress.

Reducing the effects of the fight/flight/freeze response

Helping to alleviate the physical effects of the worry alarm can significantly reduce the likelihood of the anxiety escalating.

Quick fixes

Whilst ideally you and your child will have chosen some strategies and practised them, you may not have sufficient time to do that when an issue arises. There are some 'quick fixes' that can work for children and young people, all of which involve either breathing in more oxygen or relaxing the muscles, or both.

Breathing exercises are the quickest, simplest and least intrusive way to get more oxygen into the body so that the thinking brain can work more efficiently. They can be done anywhere at any time without other people being aware. Tensing and relaxing muscles in the body can help to relieve the tension and provide the body with a calming message. It will no longer feel it is on high alert. These strategies also have the advantage of providing a distraction to help children break the worry loop of thoughts that are going around in their heads.

Noticing the signs of your child's anxiety starting is very important, as the earlier in the process you can catch it the more likely you are to alleviate the symptoms. Once it reaches crisis point, or panic attack, different measures will need to be employed, as discussed earlier.

Younger children

- Imagine you are blowing up an enormous balloon filled with air, then picture letting the air out as slowly as you can until the balloon goes flat
- Pretend to blow bubbles, or have some bubble mixture ready to use
- Pretend to change from an uncooked piece of spaghetti – straight, rigid and tense – to a cooked piece – floppy, soft and pliable
- Turn yourself into a floppy rag doll
- Play a game, see how long you can make an out-breath last by breathing out and making a gentle 'sssssssss' sound
- Lie on the floor, put hands on the tummy and feel the tummy expand on the in-breath and relax on the out-breath. If this is difficult, put something light on the tummy, a cuddly toy or a cushion, and see if it can be made to rise and fall with the breath.

Older children and young people

- Breath in deeply, as if you were smelling a lovely flower, and then blow out slowly, as if you were making a candle flame flicker but not blowing it out

- Breathe in deeply through the nose, raising your shoulders and then dropping your shoulders sharply whilst blowing breath out of the mouth
- Count down from 100 with each breath. Silently say '100' with the in-breath through the nose, then breathe out slowly through the mouth. Silently say '99' with the next breath etc. Continue until you lose count. If you wish, start again at 100
- Breathe in through the nose for a slow count of four, hold the breath for a count of four and breathe out through the mouth for a count of four. Hold the breath for a count of four. This is known as square breathing
- Relax the muscles.

Older children and young people need to develop and work on strategies that they have chosen, are comfortable with and that suit them. More detail and other strategies can be found in Parts 4 and 5.

The body has become ready for physical exercise when the worry alarm goes off, so it can be helpful to take some exercise to get rid of some of the excess energy that has developed in the body. This suits some children and young people better than others (see Chapter 8 for more discussion of the role of exercise in reducing anxiety).

Strategies suggested here and in Parts 4 and 5 will work best if they are taught and practised when you and your child are calm, so that they can be used readily by your child when they are distressed. It is tempting to want to 'leave well alone' when children are calm. However, encouraging practice to develop helpful strategies to alleviate anxiety will pay benefits in the long run.

Redefining physical discomfort associated with anxiety

Some children are distressed by the physical changes that take place when they are anxious. They may mistake these symptoms for being physically ill. If your child has physical symptoms it is important to check out with a doctor that there isn't a physical problem. Once you are sure that the symptoms are those of anxiety and not a medical issue, it can help to discuss this with your child. Redefining uncomfortable physical feelings, as described at the beginning of this chapter, involves changing the thoughts surrounding the physical feelings and seeing the physical effects as a helping strategy rather than something to be feared. This can help children and young people to appreciate that they are not in danger from their physical symptoms and reduce the likelihood of them fuelling the anxiety to higher levels.

It is interesting that all of the physiological symptoms are similar to those experienced during exercise and excitement. Help your child to consider the bodily sensations in different ways.

PHYSICAL FEELING	ANXIOUS THOUGHT	CALMING THOUGHT
Tight chest, breathlessness	I am having trouble breathing, I am going to die.	I feel like this when I run for the bus. It is uncomfortable but it will pass.
Dizziness	I am going to faint, that will be too embarrassing and I might hurt myself when I fall.	I get dizzy when I am on a roller coaster, it is a horrible feeling but it will pass.
Heart pounding, racing	There is something wrong with my heart, it is going too fast.	My heart races after I have been doing PE, it is not very pleasant but I am not in danger.
Sweating	I always get this feeling just before I have a panic attack.	I sweat when I am hot and when I exercise, it feels odd, but it is not dangerous.
Dry throat and mouth	I can't speak properly my mouth is too dry.	My throat and mouth are often dry when I wake up in the morning. It's uncomfortable but I am healthy.
Butterflies and nausea	I am going to be sick.	I also get butterflies and nausea when I am excited. It doesn't feel good but I am safe.
General bodily discomfort	I am going to have a panic attack.	I'm uncomfortable but it will pass.

TABLE 7.2 Redefining physical discomfort associated with anxiety

Managing difficult emotions

The importance of recognising, understanding and expressing emotions appropriately has been found by the authors to be crucial in working with children (Faupel et al, 2018). Although children and young people may understand the need to change thoughts and behaviours, it may be that their emotions are interfering with their ability to motivate themselves to do this. If emotions are not expressed effectively they can build up in the body and become unmanageable. They can then 'leak' out at the wrong time and in the wrong way and lead to us feeling out of control.

Neuroscience is providing evidence that when people engage in emotional experiences and then attempt to suppress their emotions there are negative effects on their health and well-being.

'Research shows that suppressing emotions actually makes them worse.'

(Rock, 2009)

It can be difficult to talk to children and young people about emotions particularly if, as a family, you are not used to doing so. Younger children may find it helpful to draw how they are feeling as they may not have the words to express emotions accurately. You can tentatively offer some words for them; for example, 'I wonder if you are feeling jealous because your brother was invited to the party and you weren't?' or 'I think you are probably disappointed that we can't go on the trip because mummy is ill'. It can be helpful for you to make your own feelings explicit (within the bounds of what it is suitable to share with children). An example of this might be 'I am feeling very proud of myself today because I cleaned the whole house', or 'I am feeling sad because I wanted to go for a walk but it is raining too hard'.

Challenging negative thoughts

Your child is likely to have developed some negative thinking patterns and to have a tendency to perceive danger and difficulty when others wouldn't. We know that different thoughts regarding the same situation will lead to different behaviours. For example,

Tom has been asked to read a poem in assembly. Negative thinking – 'I can't do it, I will make a fool of myself, everyone will laugh at me' – leads to high levels of anxiety and the likelihood that Tom will try to get out of it. Positive thoughts – 'People will think I am brave for having a go at this. It doesn't matter if I get a bit wrong, we all get things wrong sometimes. I will feel good after I have done it' – are likely to lead to Tom contributing to the assembly and learning to manage new situations. He will then be developing his strengths and resilience, rather than missing out on valuable and enjoyable experiences. Encouraging helpful thinking is something we can support as parents.

Challenging negative thoughts and teaching our children and young people to look at the evidence for their thoughts, and how likely the events are to happen in reality, can be helpful ways of changing views:

- What makes me think that will happen?
- Has that ever happened to me before?
- Have I ever seen that happen to someone else?
- How likely is it that it will happen?
- Can I imagine that anything else could happen?
- What would I think if someone else was in the same situation?
- What would someone else think if they were in the same boat?

(Adapted from Willets and Creswell, 2007)

As children and young people become more familiar with considering whether their thoughts are helpful or unhelpful you can talk about 'catching' unhelpful thoughts and 'junking' them before they do any damage. They must then be replaced with positive thoughts, as in the earlier example. In our interventions we talk about red thoughts (unhelpful) and green thoughts (helpful) and how we can change from one to the other. Younger children find this especially helpful (see Parts 4 and 5).

Our emotions are rooted in our evolutionary history to help us survive. Our survival has two main elements, avoiding dangers that threaten us (either real or perceived) and choosing opportunities that will keep us healthy. Avoiding danger demands a much more powerful emotion, because the consequences of not noticing danger (a threatening tiger, for example) might mean the end of us; whereas not noticing an opportunity to eat, drink, or become physically healthy is not as serious as there will be more opportunities in the future. This has led to a negativity bias in our thinking which is hard-wired into our brains. Rick Hanson (2013) describes negative experiences as 'Velcro', as they stick to us easily, and positive experiences as 'Teflon', as they slip off easily. Hence the negative self-talk in the car on the way home from work (' . . . and I haven't done, and I didn't manage . . . and I wish I had . . .') rather than positive self-talk ('I managed to get this done today. I did well because . . .). Now that we have to pay less attention to our survival needs and manage more complex social and emotional environments, we need to spend more time giving our mental health and emotional well-being attention. It is important to develop positive thinking habits and notice what has gone well as often as we notice what went wrong.

Devising a plan

Facing fears and changing habits takes time and is quite frightening, so don't push your child to go faster than they can. The aim is to help children put themselves in situations that they would normally avoid. Try one new behaviour at a time and/or gradually stay for longer periods of time in situations that have previously been avoided.

Sometimes activities appear to be too difficult, like a mountain to climb. As with climbing a mountain, if you look at the top and think about getting there it will seem impossible. However, if you break it down into small steps it becomes more manageable; for example, 'If I can just get to . . . .'

It is important to help your child plan small steps to change. Break the activity down into small pieces and try to achieve one at a time. Do not move on to the second step before the first one has been accomplished successfully. You could ask your child to imagine they are a tiny mouse with a large piece of cheese to eat. The mouse wants to eat the cheese, cannot eat it all at once but manages a bit at a time.

Emergency tool box

When you have been through some of the processes outlined above you will begin to see what helps your child at different stages of their anxiety. It is helpful to devise an 'emergency tool box' with your child, using suggestions and strategies that they have chosen.

We have varied the name we have given to this set of strategies to suit the child, young person or group of youngsters we have worked with. Sometimes we call it an 'emotional first aid kit', a 'bag of tricks' or even 'magic spells'. You could choose a name that appeals to your youngster or get him or her to make a choice. This can then be drawn or, if preferred, written down. Alternative strategies are then available for the early signs and signals, through to the more extreme stages of anxiety (see Parts 4 and 5).

Building resilience

Learning how to manage the obstacles that life throws in our paths is a normal part of growing up. It is a crucial part of our development and learning and helps us to recognise our strengths, build confidence and feel competent in the world. Resilience is a key element in our social emotional well-being and contributes greatly to good mental health.

It is very easy to be overprotective with our children because we want to keep them safe, but being overprotective may impact on a child's ability to take some risks, make mistakes and learn from them.

Resilience skills grow out of strong and supportive relationships that children develop with their families and close friends.

How to help

Do
- give children independence to do things for themselves and learn by their mistakes
- allow them to be unhappy at times; it is a vital learning experience
- demonstrate that failure isn't a catastrophe; your love and affection are unconditional
- praise children for effort rather than attainment
- spend individual quality time with your child
- identify and reinforce your child's strengths
- nurture a positive self-view
- keep things in perspective and adopt a positive outlook
- lead by example when dealing with your own setbacks and disappointments
- adopt a growth mindset approach – we can all make progress if we put in the effort.

Do not
- solve all their problems for them – we all need to learn by our mistakes
- stop them experiencing frustrations or taking risks
- overprotect them from difficulties and setbacks
- become overly obsessed with safety
- create a timetable that is full of structured activities; time for free play is an important self-development tool

- encourage perfectionism – your love is unconditional
- provide a negative role model.

Young Minds (UK) offers support for helping your child to build resilience (see Useful websites).

Parents as role models

We know that children learn from watching others and are particularly affected by those close to them. As parents we are therefore acting as role models for our children and young people. They are far more likely to be influenced by watching how we manage our own difficulties than by telling them what they should do. Anxious children and anxious adults tend to think about things in a similar way. If we can set an example to our children by challenging our own negative thoughts, trying to see the world as a less threatening place and attempting to spend less time avoiding situations we perceive as threatening, it will help our children to do the same. The cycle below shows how easy it is for our own anxieties to contribute towards our children's anxieties.

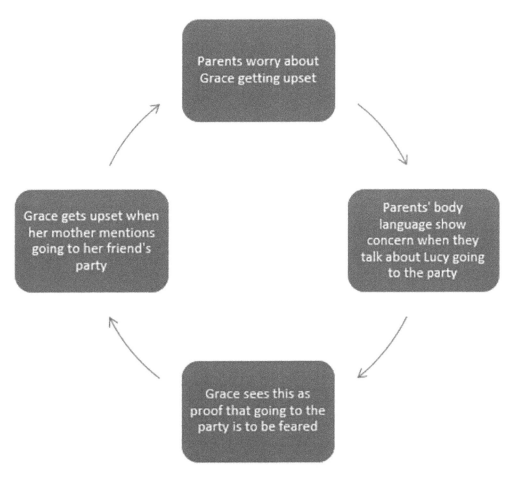

FIGURE 7.3 The effect of parents' anxiety

Covering up our own anxieties, however, may not be helpful for children. Children and young people often feel that they are the only ones who feel as they do and that this makes them odd and different. They may not be aware that everyone has anxieties and feels worried and scared some of the time. It is important for us as adults to show that having anxiety is normal and that there are ways of managing it so that anxiety does not interfere with our everyday lives.

Ask yourself the following questions:

- Do you find it difficult to talk about and express your feelings?
- Do you consider the world to be a threatening place at times?
- Do you have times when you can't think clearly and rationally (fight or flight mode)?
- Do you suffer from any of the physical effects of anxiety and worry?
- Do you find yourself thinking negative and catastrophic thoughts?
- Do you avoid situations you are worried about?

If you are answering yes to several of these questions you may want to think about how you are managing your own anxiety whilst supporting your child with theirs. It is important that we look after ourselves as well as our children and young people. This is not always easy as a busy parent, but is very important if we are to demonstrate and teach our children how to manage themselves well. In Chapter 8 you will find suggestions for a healthy lifestyle and how to look after yourself. This will reduce the likelihood that you will suffer from too much anxiety and worry and enable you to support your children and young people effectively. If your anxiety is negatively affecting your life, you might wish to seek professional help for yourself.

Whilst parents can do a great deal to support their children, they are likely to be more successful if they can enlist support from others. The saying 'it takes a village to raise a child' is a sentiment with which the authors agree.

It may be possible to enlist help from a range of community members, of which school staff are likely to be very important. Discussing your concerns and enlisting help from the school can be key.

There will, however, be situations in which a child with the best-informed parents and school staff still requires specialist mental health support. Should you, as a parent, feel out of your depth with your own child, we advise you to seek specialist support.

Conclusion

Parents are the greatest influence on their children and can help enormously when children show signs of anxiety. Early effective support reduces the likelihood that mental health difficulties will occur later in life.

There are positive consequences for children and young people when parents are well and taking care of their own emotional, social, physical and intellectual needs. Emotional energy can be depleted with the stresses and strains of being a busy parent. It is important that parents take care of their own emotional needs in order to be able to support their child effectively. If parents look after their own mental health, not only will this provide a good role model for children and young people but it will also ensure that parents have the internal strength and resources to help their children.

Children will usually benefit from their parents working collaboratively with school staff, so making positive relationships will pay dividends. If parents and school staff find they are not able to help, specialist advice should be sought.

Summary

Introduction

Separation anxiety

Panic attacks

Interventions

➤ Anxiety processes
➤ Identifying triggers
➤ Identifying early signs and signals
➤ Reducing the effect of the fight/flight response
➤ Managing difficult emotions
➤ Challenging negative thoughts
➤ Developing a plan
➤ The emergency tool kit

Building resilience

Parents as role models

Conclusion

Creating a healthy lifestyle

Introduction

When we are caring for a child or young person with anxiety it is important to pay attention to their basic needs as a foundation for emotional well-being, as minds and bodies are inextricably linked. The age-old phrase 'a healthy mind in a healthy body' is often used to express the theory that physical exercise is important for emotional and psychological well-being. It is now recognised that many other aspects of our lifestyles can also affect our physical and mental health. This chapter will explore different areas of a child or young person's life where it could be helpful to make changes that may reduce the severity of anxiety.

Parents are the adults who have most control over their children's lifestyle, although this control naturally decreases as children mature into young people. Parents of young children may be able to make positive changes over the child's lifestyle, whilst parents of older children and young people may need to negotiate lifestyle changes. It is also difficult to change the lifestyle of one member of the family and not others. The authors have worked with families who changed the lifestyle for the whole family, and everyone has benefited as a result.

All change is difficult, whether it involves feelings, thoughts, behaviours, or physical activity. We learn ways of managing ourselves with which we feel comfortable and familiar, even if they are not necessarily the healthiest options for us. Change can be uncomfortable, feel threatening, take time and need support. If children or young people have developed unhealthy lifestyles they will need sensitive help to unlearn bad habits, develop habits that support their emotional health and reduce anxiety.

Whilst primarily written for parents, professionals reading this chapter may be able to find suggestions to assist the parents with whom they work.

Maslow's hierarchy of need

Maslow's hierarchy of need reminds us that we have a range of needs that are important to all of us to achieve physical and mental health. As can be seen from the figure below, a healthy lifestyle needs to incorporate all needs: physiological, safety, love and belonging, self-esteem and self-actualisation. Whilst this is clearly an oversimplification, and

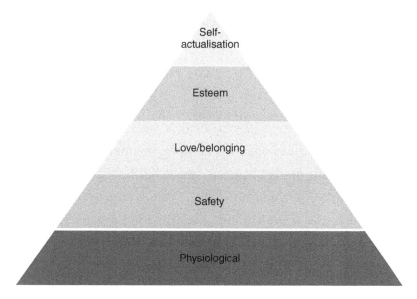

FIGURE 8.1 Maslow's hierarchy of need

many of the levels overlap, it is a helpful structure for us to use to consider aspects of lifestyle that support physical and emotional health.

When we are caring for or working with an anxious child we are unlikely to be successful if the child is facing genuine dangers in life. When the child's basic physiological and safety needs are met, they will have more attention available for emotional needs. A child who feels love and belonging is more likely to have the emotional energy and strength to work on lifestyle changes. Whilst parents create the basis of this security, schools also have a lot to offer in creating the space in which a child's physiological, safety and belonging needs are met and in supporting self-esteem. Only with all these in place can a person achieve their potential (self-actualisation). We will now look at these areas in greater detail.

Physiological needs

Physical health

It is very difficult to maintain emotional health when physical health is poor, so ensuring that everything possible is done to promote physical health will assist in helping an anxious child. Children and young people, like adults, will be more prone to anxiety in periods of physical illness, even when that illness is as mild as a cold.

Sometimes it is not easy to separate physical and emotional symptoms, particularly when they are expressed as bodily discomfort. It is important to check out any physical difficulties with the GP to ensure that a physical problem is not being treated as if it were emotional. Children may need to receive appropriate treatment for bodily ills, so, before assuming that any symptoms are emotional, we need to exclude a physical cause.

Exercise

Exercise offers protective benefits to mental health, with some studies showing it to be as effective a treatment as medication; for example, Blumenthal et al (2012). Our bodies have evolved to be active and many children find it hard to sit still for long periods. It is also very difficult to enjoy good mental health if you are physically tense, which is often the case with chronic anxiety. Exercise increases the hormones that make us feel good and helps us to get rid of pent up adrenaline that has been released when the 'worry alarm' (fight/flight response) goes off in our brains.

Whilst some children and young people readily run about in play and sports, others are unwilling to exercise. The main aim here is to find a type of exercise that is enjoyable for the child or young person, whether this is football, yoga, climbing, walking, running, dance or any other active pursuit. Initially the young person may need a lot of support and encouragement to try new things, about which they may be anxious. However, if young people are able to find a form of exercise which they enjoy, then maintaining the activity will be much easier.

Depending on the type of exercise chosen, there may be additional benefits such as being outdoors and appreciating nature, increasing social contacts through sports or societies, or spending time together with the family.

Diet and nutrition

Eating well also plays a strong role in maintaining our physical and mental health. Whilst there are no 'miracle cures', a healthy diet together with exercise increases mental well-being. The NHS encourages us to eat plenty of fruit and vegetables and high fibre or wholegrain starchy carbohydrates (potatoes, bread, rice, pasta), smaller quantities of beans, pulses, fish, eggs, meat, and small quantities of dairy products. This varied diet will provide the vitamins and food classes we need. Iron deficiency can be a problem for adolescents as their bodies are changing very rapidly. People can get iron by eating foods such as meat and dark-green, leafy vegetables. For details see www.nhsinform.scot.

Sugar

Children with anxiety may crave simple carbohydrates and sugar which increase the hormones that make them feel good in the short term. However, as sugar levels drop the desire to eat more carbohydrates and sugar increases, creating another difficult cycle to break. Comfort eating can develop as a coping strategy for the pain associated with difficult feelings.

Complex carbohydrates can also increase the level of hormones needed to help improve how we feel, but are not associated with the highs and lows of simple sugars as they keep the blood sugar level over time. This reduces the cravings associated with eating high levels of sugar and simple carbohydrates.

If a child or young person has developed unhealthy eating habits these will not be easy to break, but the sooner the habits are broken the better. Switching from sugary foods to whole-grain breads and cereals may well have a calming effect on the body. Dark chocolate has been found to be much healthier for us than milk chocolate.

Hydration

The importance of keeping well hydrated has become better known in the last ten years. It is not always easy to recognise when a child is dehydrated, and it can be manifested in symptoms other than thirst; tiredness, hunger and lack of concentration, for example. The hunger associated with dehydration increases the craving for carbohydrates and sugary foods, which in turn increases insulin levels and means we need to take in more water. This can become another difficult cycle to break.

Children need to be encouraged to drink water regularly. Drinks with caffeine in them are stimulants and also reduce the level of hydration, so should be discouraged. Youngsters can be taught to have a drink of water when they begin to feel anxious and irritable. This may be a good distractor as well as helping to maintain hydration.

Omega-3

There are also some fatty acids which are known to be helpful in maintaining and improving the mood. Research is showing that increasing the amount of the essential fatty acid, Omega 3, in the diet can help to improve our physical and mental well-being. It can be found in oily fish such as salmon, mackerel and sardines. Omega 3, in a slightly different format, is also found in pecans, hazelnuts and walnuts if fish does not appeal to your taste. Eating salmon instead of white fish and nuts instead of crisps can help to maintain the levels of Omega 3.

Stimulants

Avoiding drinks which contain stimulants is beneficial to well-being. The caffeine present in tea, coffee and some fizzy drinks can significantly impair sleep and increase irritability. These drinks may also contain high levels of sugar and lead to the cravings described above. It is helpful to teach youngsters to choose drinks that are both sugar- and caffeine-free.

Tobacco can also be classified as a stimulant, although smokers often say that they smoke to calm down. It is likely that the calming effect is associated with the relief of withdrawal symptoms from the drug as well as the regular and deep breathing associated with smoking. The addiction to nicotine will lead to further cravings, irritability and anxiety as the effect wears off and the body craves more to keep the drug which it has become dependent on at a comfortable physical level. All stimulants act as a poison in the body and reduce the ability to function in harmony between mind and body. Parents can set a good example by not smoking, or quitting smoking themselves. The earlier a young person starts to smoke, the harder it will be to quit. Obviously the best answer is not to start at all, but if a young person has started to smoke they will need help to cease.

Sleep hygiene

Sleep is often difficult for children and young people with anxiety. Either getting to sleep or waking in the early hours of the morning is commonly experienced. Being anxious about not being able to get to sleep can make the situation worse. An unpleasant cycle can be formed, which is difficult to break: reduced sleep leads to more anxiety, which in turn leads to reduced sleep. Long-term sleep problems can lead to irritability, disruptive and impulsive behaviours and lack of concentration. It is very important to establish good sleep habits and routines for children.

Space to sleep

The bedroom needs to be identified as a place to rest, relax and sleep. It is better not to have access to TV, PlayStation, or other electronic devices in the bedroom as these tend to stimulate the brain rather than relax it. Teenagers often live in their bedrooms, so if possible it is helpful to separate different areas of the room for study, leisure and sleep. Mobile phones and iPads should be left downstairs at night and not used on the bed during the day. The bed needs to be kept specifically as a place to rest and sleep. Bedrooms should be cool and dark as this is the body's preferred sleep environment, although younger children may feel comforted by a night light.

Bedtime routines

Going to bed and, even more importantly, getting up at the same time every day helps the body to get into a regular sleep/wake pattern. Teenagers will often sleep late at weekends, leading to 'Sunday night insomnia' when they cannot sleep because their body has had sufficient sleep over the weekend. Hard as it may seem, getting up at weekends not much later than on school days will significantly help with the sleep/wake pattern.

Having a specific routine before bed can also encourage the body to recognise that it is time to relax and become calm in preparation for sleep. Sleep routines need to include relaxing and calming activities rather than stimulating ones. Children and young people need an hour of calming activities before they prepare to sleep. Avoid activities that are overstimulating during this hour; for example, physical exercise, or exciting play with siblings, friends, or parents. It can be tempting to use games on screens to calm children and young people, but it is now known that this has the opposite effect as it stimulates our brains rather than calms them.

For a young child who wakes regularly in the night it is important to establish a consistent routine which does not reinforce the behaviour. The child should be taken back to bed with little fuss or attention. Avoid chatting, reading a story, providing food or drink, or telling them off. For some children even being told off may provide some adult attention, and if that is what they crave this may be counterproductive. It is more important to ensure they have positive individual attention during the day. Sticker charts may help to encourage children to stay in bed through the night. A small reward can be agreed with the child beforehand.

Check the following if your child is struggling to sleep.

Have they had a stimulating drink before bed (drinks with caffeine in them, for example)?

Have they been over-stimulated in the hour before bedtime?

Are there stimulating games, activities in the bedroom?

Are parents reinforcing their child's bad sleep patterns; for example, allowing them to come down and sit with the family if they cannot sleep (a 'payoff')?

Is the bedroom a good temperature?

Is the bedroom kept as a place to relax and sleep?

Is the child comfortable in bed; i.e., mattress, pillow, warmth, sleep wear?

Is something or someone disturbing the child's sleep (siblings, sounds and lights)?

Is he/she hungry or thirsty?

Does the child have any allergies that may be affecting them (for example, duck down in the duvet, feathers in the pillow)?

Are the light levels appropriate for the child?

Does the child need a calming activity in the bedroom to help them relax; listening to an audio story, reading a book, cuddly toys, gentle music, a 'special' blanket associated just with sleep?

If there are severe sleep difficulties that do not respond to consistent bedtime routines and good sleep-health patterns, it may be advisable to consult the GP regarding a referral to a sleep clinic.

Relaxation

The pressures of daily life in the modern world can mean that busy families have little time for relaxation, especially with many adults and children opting to spend free time online or watching television. Whilst this has its advantages in moderation, it does mean that children and young people often miss out on conversation, playing games and simply being together as a family. If you find that there is not enough down-time in your family, with games and fun, it may be worth setting aside some time every day or every week for family fun. Children especially need screen-free relaxed time in the period before bed time.

Some anxious children may require more formal tuition in how to relax. They may need help to develop effective strategies to keep their stress levels within the normal range. This is likely to involve simple breathing exercises, as described in Chapter 7. For more detailed advice on relaxation exercises, see Part 4.

Safety

Physical safety

Clearly if children are not physically safe it does not make sense to address their anxiety as if it were unwarranted. Therefore it is always important to check whether a child has any reasonable fears which need to be addressed by the adults responsible. It is the duty of a parent to keep their child safe, and if professionals have doubts about a child's safety they must follow child protection procedures. Any issues of physical safety should be resolved as a matter of urgency, allowing a child or young person the security to address emotional needs.

Technology and safety

Children and young people are now growing up, interacting and learning within a digital world which is quite different from the world that most parents and carers knew as they were developing. Easy access to social media may be affecting mental health and well-being of our children, who spend more time on mobile phones, tablets and gaming than ever before. Whilst there are some benefits – such as keeping in touch with friends and online support – there are also risks in having to be constantly available and vigilant to what is being posted.

'Vulnerability also arises through the instant sharing of personal information, the difficulties with retracting personal information, and the potential for misreading social situations and causing unintentional distress.'

(Ecorys/Young Minds, 2018)

Some children are more at risk than others from online bullying or pressure to conform.

'A growing body of evidence suggests that online and offline resilience are linked.'

(Digital Age Conference, Parentzone, 2018)

Setting rules and boundaries around technology use may feel somewhat daunting in terms of deciding appropriate expectations, but it is important. For older youngsters this may require a family conversation about the reasons for these rules, which are then applied consistently to everyone in the family. Some parents we have worked with have found it very hard to restrict their youngsters' use of the internet because they themselves are unwilling to restrict their own use. However, it may be necessary to agree periods of time when access to the internet is switched off for everyone.

You may want to consider the following areas of technology use, to help you decide what is important for you, your children and your family:

- Time restrictions: deciding when technology can and can't be used and for how long. Consider at night, during study time, when it is impolite; family meals or when there are visitors, for example.
- Place restrictions: consider bedrooms, study quarters, at school.
- Content restrictions: consider what is age-appropriate material for your child(ren), discuss it with them and, if necessary, use parental controls.

When used wisely, technology is a great addition to our way of life. It is important to help children and young people develop resilience online as well as offline and be aware of our parental responsibilities in keeping our children safe and healthy.

Love and belonging

Perhaps it goes without saying that we all need to know we are loved. A parent's first duty is to love their child, and a loved child will be more resilient to life's challenges. The child will usually belong first in the family and, second, to school. Schools offering a positive sense of belonging also contribute greatly to well-being. Thus parents need to be sure that their child is loved, knows they are loved and belongs both at home and school. Teenagers may appear not to value their parents' love but need it just as much. This may be a period of life in which parents need to continue to give, sometimes with little acknowledgement, until the young person is mature enough to recognise their parents' goodwill.

Friendships

Friendships bring joy and happiness and sometimes conflict. Friendships enable children to learn new skills and build their relationships. Whilst some children and young people seem to be forever in a whirlwind of social life, some anxious children and young people may need encouragement to join in with social engagements. Anxious children are less likely to engage socially both at school and at home due to their fears, which can lead them to hide away, not make conversation and fail to smile or make eye contact. They may need extra help to make friends.

Parents may find they need to organise outings and 'play dates' for younger children. As children grow up they may need support in finding ways to manage the inevitable conflicts that occur in relationships. All of these are skills that will help children and young people to enjoy others, have fun and manage the difficulties we inevitably encounter through life.

School and community

Children spend many hours at school and have little ability to choose how they spend their time there. Schools can make a huge difference to students by helping them feel cared for and that they belong to their school community (see Chapters 4 and 5). If your child is unhappy or anxious at school, engage school staff in working with you to help your child or young person.

Some children and young people experiencing anxiety are likely to benefit from support to develop social and friendship skills. If you think your child does not have the skills to make friendships and you are unable to help your child sufficiently, speak with school staff about how he or she can be helped in school.

Self-esteem

Building your child's self-esteem is an important part of their upbringing. They need to know they are loved, valued and important, regardless of their abilities.

Perfectionism

Anxious people tend to be perfectionists. Children with a mistaken belief that it is important to get things perfect all the time may avoid activities and tasks, rather than try but not meet their own exacting standards. Perfectionism can lead to a fear of failure, with children refusing to attempt things they may not do well. They may be anxious about failing in the future or worry about things they have 'failed' at in the past. They may have difficulties starting a task because it may go wrong (procrastination) or finishing a task because it is never good enough. Inevitably we are never going to be perfect, so perfectionists risk feeling depressed and finding everything a struggle.

Here are some suggestions to combat perfectionism:

- Help to develop resilience by letting children get things wrong
- Explain that mistakes make your brain stronger and enable us to learn
- Play games that involve cooperation rather than competition; for example, Dinosaur Escape (available to buy online)
- Spend individual time with your child doing things together which do not turn out 'perfectly'
- Find activities that have several 'correct' answers
- Encourage your child to enjoy the process of doing something rather than the outcome. For ideas consider GoZen's *Healthy Perfectionist Activity Book*
- Remind children of the things they used not to be able to do when they were younger and can now succeed at; for example, riding a bike, writing, reading, skipping, dressing themselves. Ask them to consider whether they managed it perfectly the first time they tried it and, if not, how they became confident and competent at it.

For children and young people to maintain and develop their emotional well-being it is important that they do not avoid all the situations they find difficult, but are encouraged to try and keep practising. Thomas Edison invented the light bulb after a long process of getting it wrong and learning from his mistakes until he succeeded. The following quote summarises this approach to life:

> 'I have not failed. I've just found 10,000 ways that won't work.'

Self-compassion and acceptance

Self-compassion is about being kind to ourselves. This is something children need to be helped to do, by experiencing kindness from others and seeing the adults around them 'model' treating themselves with compassion. As a parent you might find this hard to do as many of us treat ourselves more negatively than we would our friends and family. Self-compassion is not about being selfish; it is about not criticising ourselves harshly and about accepting ourselves.

We have a tendency to believe what we tell ourselves, especially if we tell ourselves the same thing repeatedly. Neural imaging has shown that:

> 'The neurons that fire together wire together.'
>
> (Hebb, 1949)

97

In other words, the more often we think a particular thought the more likely we are to think it again, as we have created that pathway in the brain. Equally, if children continually hear (or tell themselves) that they are 'naughty', 'bad', 'clumsy' or 'wrong' they will develop that picture of themselves.

As described in the previous chapter, it is human nature to judge ourselves harshly as we have evolved to notice what needs to be put right rather than the things that are going well.

Children can be helped to develop positive ways of thinking about themselves, based on how the people around them react. Encourage children to avoid negative self-talk (for example, 'I can't do this, I'm stupid') and replace it with positive self-talk ('I can't do this on my own yet, I need some help').

Equally, some emotions are painful and difficult to manage, but learning to observe them and accept them without judgement will help children and young people to manage them better. They need to learn that there is nothing wrong with feeling angry, anxious, sad, or fearful. It is how we behave when we have those feelings that we need to take responsibility for (see Chapter 1 for further information on acceptance and commitment theory).

Teaching children and young people simple 'check-in' strategies can help raise awareness of difficulties before they become unmanageable and can be really helpful.

Emotional check-in:

- How am I doing?
- Is there anything bothering me at the moment?
- How stressed do I feel?
- Do I need to do anything differently in order to reduce my stress and help me to feel better at the moment?

(Adapted from Brotheridge, 2017)

Self-actualisation

What is this life if, full of care,

We have no time to stand and stare.

(W.H. Davies, 1911)

Self-actualisation is the highest point of Maslow's hierarchy and is about us reaching our full potential, creatively, academically and spiritually. It is something we work on throughout our lives. Children can be introduced to these aspects of growth from an early age.

The arts and creativity

Young children are naturally creative, but somehow as we grow up most of us gain inhibitions and lose our confidence in our creative abilities. It is helpful to encourage children and young people to enjoy being creative in whatever way appeals to them, whether this be drawing, music, dance, poetry, or any other art form. The aim here is not necessarily for the child or young person to produce anything, but simply to enjoy the activity and express themselves.

Spiritual well-being

Spirituality involves appreciating being part of a wider universe, feeling connected, having purpose, faith, beliefs and values. It involves our in-built curiosity about the world and leads us to ask questions such as 'Where do we come from?', 'Who am I?' and 'Why am I here?' If you have religious beliefs you will have an approach to these questions, and you may belong to a group with shared beliefs, rituals and practices.

If you are not religious it might be tempting to think that spirituality is for adults rather than children and young people. However, the concepts of awe and wonder appear in the British National Curriculum and children's spirituality is being increasingly recognised as important for good mental health. Spirituality does not always involve religious beliefs; it may be simply a sense of wonder about natural and human beauty. Taking part with community practices in celebrating festivals helps children to develop a sense of belonging and a deeper sense of identity and self-worth.

Parents can help their children and young people appreciate the beauties and wonders of the world by spending time together in natural surroundings, paying attention to the wonders of the world and feeling gratitude for the good things in life (see Seden, 2018).

Conclusion

A healthy lifestyle enhances both physical and mental health. Maslow's hierarchy of need helps us to understand the importance of each of the various aspects of our development and the needs that children have, to mature into strong and resilient adults. A healthy lifestyle will not 'cure' anxiety, but it will significantly improve the probability of recovery and improve quality of life by reducing symptoms.

Summary

Introduction

Maslow's hierarchy

Physiological needs

➤ Physical health
➤ Exercise
➤ Diet and nutrition
➤ Sleep hygiene
➤ Relaxation

Safety

➤ Physical safety
➤ Technology

Love and belonging

➤ Friendships
➤ School and community

Self-esteem

➤ Perfectionism
➤ Self-compassion

Self-actualisation

➤ The arts and creativity
➤ Spirituality

Conclusion

Part 4
Practical interventions

Ten-week intervention programme for small groups: session plans

Introduction

Working with anxious children and young people in a small group requires judgement and sensitivity. An adult taking on work with vulnerable children should be sure they have the skills and support necessary to help the children and young people gain confidence and develop skills. It may sometimes be possible to have a second adult supporting the group. This may be particularly helpful if the facilitator is not known to the children but the second adult is familiar to them. We would also suggest reading the relevant part of Chapter 6 before beginning the work.

These sessions have been designed for small groups of children or young people who are of similar ages and with similar difficulties. Working with a group has a number of advantages: the students can have fun together, realise that they are not the only ones with issues, gain support and ideas from one another, and there is less pressure on each student than in an individual setting. However, there is not always an obvious group of students requiring the intervention at the same time and it is possible for a parent or professional to work through the sessions with an individual child. Equally, the sessions require only minimal adaptation to be used with whole classes as part of emotional literacy education.

Typically, the sessions include a lively, appealing and short video clip, which can be easily found on the internet, to introduce the students to the concept being taught. Where possible we have included more than one clip, so that the facilitator can choose the one most suited to the age and understanding of the particular group. Some of these video clips are books being read aloud. If adults have access to these books they may prefer to read them with the children. There is discussion around the concept and tasks to consolidate the learning.

The sessions have been written to help the facilitator work methodically through an introduction to both a theoretical understanding of anxiety and a range of possible strategies for the students to trial. Students will need to find the strategies that suit them best, practise them and then use them in daily life. With this in mind, the sessions each have a task attached for the students to carry out between sessions.

A level of trust is required to allow students to open up honestly in these sessions, therefore ground rules need to be set and adhered to. We recommend that the introductory session be used even if the students taking part know each other in advance. The importance of showing respect should be emphasised. Early on an evolutionary theory of anxiety is introduced, to help students recognise the useful role anxiety plays in life when kept in check. Students are encouraged to recognise and name their emotions to begin to take charge of them. Cognitive-behavioural approaches are used to help students identify how their conscious thoughts can change their feelings and behaviours. A wide variety of strategies are introduced and the students are invited to select those which work for them individually. In the last session, each child or young person develops their own 'emergency first aid kit' with the strategies that they have found to be helpful for them.

Outlines of each of the ten sessions are provided with a suggested script for each session, shown in quotation marks. There is no need to use the wording exactly; it is for guidance only. An outline of all ten sessions is provided so that the shape of the ten-week intervention can be identified from the beginning. The worksheets and weekly activities can be found in Appendices 1 and 2.

The work is planned so that professionals can deliver enjoyable, well-structured sessions with easily available resources. A session can be completed in 30 minutes, although 45 minutes is preferable as a longer session allows for more in-depth discussion and practice.

We have found that the group participants enjoy thinking of a name for the group; the Rocket Club, the Unicorns, the Explorers, for example. In each case you can then name the tasks and 'emergency first aid kit' accordingly. For the Rocket Club we set weekly missions and developed an emergency tool kit. For the Unicorns we set weekly quests and developed a velvet pouch of magic spells. For the Explorers we set weekly adventures and developed an emergency back pack of essential supplies. In the session plans and worksheets provided we have used weekly missions throughout for ease of presentation, but you will be able to customise these to your own design on the e-resources.

At the end of your sessions it is good practice to review the progress of each child/ young person individually and consider if he or she needs further interventions. You may also wish to plan in some follow-up sessions for the group, to provide reminders and reinforcement as the participants are trying out the strategies they have learnt.

Outline of a ten-week programme

Session 1: Getting to know each other

- Building rapport and writing ground rules
- Understanding that everyone gets anxious sometimes.

Session 2: What are worry and anxiety?

- Evolutionary perspective
- Identifying worry words.

Session 3: How does anxiety make us feel?

- Physical changes
- Where do we feel anxiety in our bodies?

Session 4: How can we help ourselves feel better?

- Calming down the amygdala
- Relaxation, exercise, calming.

Session 5: Using our strengths to help us.

- Identifying personal strengths
- Applying personal strengths.

Session 6: Naming and taming emotions.

- Recognising emotions
- Naming emotions.

Session 7: Changing how we think.

- Identifying unhelpful (red) thoughts
- Changing red thoughts to helpful (green) thoughts.

Session 8: Doing things differently.

- Identifying unhelpful (red) behaviour
- Changing red behaviour to helpful (green) behaviour.

Session 9: Choosing the strategies that work for us.

- Identifying individual favourite strategies
- Creating an aide memoire; for example, an emergency tool kit.

Session 10: Review and celebration.

- Review what we have learnt
- Celebration and certificates.

Session 1. Getting to know each other

Materials required

YouTube videos:

Younger and middle students: Harold B Wigglebottom 'Listen about courage and fear' https://www.youtube.com/watch?v=g6mlDp_FH7U

Older students: Flocabulary 'Managing worry and anxiety for kids' https://www.youtube.com/watch?v=I7g8Atv27Q8

An ice-breaker or name-learning game suitable for the age group. For examples see:

https://www.youtube.com/watch?v=OzKY5YHnOTg and

https://www.youtube.com/watch?v=TwcAl69YSyI&t=10s

Mission sheet 2.1 (Smiling), one per student

Introduction

If the children do not know each other, begin with introductions or a name-learning game (see examples above).

'We are going to be meeting together for the next few weeks to learn about how we can help ourselves be happy and calm and to worry less. We will play some games, learn new things and try out new activities. We will be sharing how we feel and so we need to be especially kind to each other. We need to agree some rules about what we do and how we speak to each other, so we all feel comfortable to share. What are the things we need to be sure of, to feel OK talking with each other? What rules can we agree to help us?'

The children may need help with this, so prompt them. You should end up with three to five rules along the following lines.

- Confidentiality outside the group
- Listen to each other
- Try to say helpful (not hurtful) things
- Try to be honest.

Choose a name for the group.

Discuss what the children would like to call their group; for example, the Rocket Club, the Unicorn Club, the Explorers.

Teaching activity

'Now we are going to practise some activities in which we speak about ourselves and everyone follows the ground rules' (for example, children speak in pairs to find something they *both* like doing out of school, which they then share with the group). 'Well done everyone. Now remember, this is how we are going to speak with each other all the times we are in this group, with respect. Now we are going to watch a short video. Look at it carefully because it is going to help us think about how we can be happier, braver people and to worry less'.

Show video.

'What made Joey/Harold anxious? Have you ever had worries like that? Remember, we are following our ground rules here, being honest, listening to each other and saying helpful things. Are those the worries people here feel? Or do we have other worries – what are some of them? What helped Joey/Harold? Might some of those things help us?'

Discussion

'Do you think other people get worried? Do adults get worried? Does everybody worry about the same things? Are you brave about some things that frighten other people? There are things we can do to help us when we worry. Does anyone have any ideas about what helps them, but wasn't on the video we watched?' Encourage discussion, help children to understand everyone worries – some more than others.

Conclusion

Finish with a positive activity; pass a smile, for example. Simply say that we're going to pass a smile around the circle. Start this off by passing a big smile to the person sitting to your left, and then encourage it all the way around.

Mission

'This week's mission is to smile at everyone from the group whenever you see each other. If you are feeling brave you can smile at other people too. See if they smile back. Make a note of who you smiled at and whether they smiled back.' Hand out mission sheets. 'Bring your mission sheet back next week because we will be talking about it.'

Session 2. What are worry and anxiety?

Materials required

YouTube videos:

Middle-older students: 'Fight or flight, the stress response'

https://www.youtube.com/watch?v=JtSP7gJuRFE

Younger-middle students: 'Anxiety: why humans experience anxiety'

https://www.youtube.com/watch?v=7W_rlrwH-BE

Worksheet 1.1 (Worry words)

Worksheet 1.2 (Fear thermometer)

Mission sheet 2.2 (Trying out an idea), one per student

Review

'Who smiled and said hello to people in the week? How did it go? Did anyone have someone smile back? Did it feel good?' Allow discussion.

'Did people worry about smiling at others? Did you need to be brave to do it? These sessions are about worrying just the right amount, not too much and not too little.'

Introduction

'Everyone worries sometimes. Anxiety is the emotion we feel when we are worrying. Worry is helpful at times, if it prompts us to do our homework or clean our teeth. Sometimes we worry so much that it is not helpful for us any- more, and we need to do something to change. That's what these sessions are about. Think about a time you were too worried about something and tell the person next to you what you thought, felt and did.'

Pause for thinking, talking and then ask one or two to share. 'How did it feel to be anxious? Was it uncomfortable to feel anxious? Did it change what you did? Did being anxious help in any way? Did it make you do something better or worse? How did it feel when it stopped?' Allow discussion.

'We are going to spend some time together thinking about and working on anxiety, to help us feel more comfortable and to learn ways to stop it getting in the way of us doing helpful things.'

Teaching activity

Show video.

'Suppose you are in the country and as you walk down a trail you see a snake in your path. What do you do? Throw a rock? Run away? Or freeze until it goes away? Those choices are what we call the *fight, flight or freeze* responses. When there is something dangerous to us, those can be really useful things to do.

'This is helpful if it is a real physical danger – and when we were living in caves surrounded by wild animals the danger was usually physical and very real. What about if we are afraid of a spelling test? Whilst a little bit of anxiety can make us practice beforehand and be alert in the test, too much is not good for us and may make us angry (the fight response), refuse to do it/feel too ill to practise or take the test (flight), or just go blank in the middle of the test (freeze). Long-term anxiety can make us unwell and unhappy.'

Discussion

Collect from the group all the words they have for worry and anxiety. Supplement if necessary from Worksheet 1.1 (Worry words). Write them up on a whiteboard/flip chart. 'Now we have a lot of words about worrying. We are each going to pick out four words that apply to us and order them from slightly worried, through more worried, very worried and the worst worry you can imagine. Once you have decided, you can write them down beside the relevant face on your individual fear thermometer.'

Share Worksheet 1.2.

For older students, you might decide simply to have them choose more words and then rank them.

'Now let's each think of one or two things that help each of us when we are feeling worried.' Have some simple suggestions ready in case few are offered; for example, go for a walk, get a drink of water, tell a friend/adult, ask a teacher to help, pet the dog, take deep breaths, think happy thoughts, ask for a hug. Also thinking about 'what is' instead of 'what if', tell yourself 'It's OK to be afraid – if you aren't afraid you can't be brave'. Refer back to video in session 1.

Conclusion

'Everyone worries and feels anxious at times, and that can be a good thing if it helps us to do things we need to do. Too much worry feels bad and doesn't help us. We are going to spend the next few sessions together learning about things that can help us. We have just shared some ideas of simple things that some of us are already doing. Maybe you already have something that helps you a lot. Maybe you just got an idea from someone else.'

Mission

'Now I want you to choose one idea to practise this week. When we meet again I will ask you all to tell me how the practising went and if it really helped you. Write or draw and label on your mission sheet one thing you will try this week.' Give out mission sheets and check that all children have drawn or written what they will do. Keep a note of each in case they forget to return them.

Session 3. How does anxiety make us feel?

Materials required

YouTube videos:

For younger children: 'Wilma Jean the Worry Machine' book or video:

https://www.youtube.com/watch?v=gpAijfP99Ng

For older students: 'Fear vs. Anxiety – What's the difference?'

https://www.youtube.com/watch?v=Ov5E6syVppI

Body Template, print one per student from http://printables.atozteacherstuff.com/download/all-about-me/body_template.pdf

Mission sheet 2.3 (Noticing how our bodies feel), one per student

Review/introduction

'How did you all get on with your mission? Did the thing you tried help?' Take feedback from each student. 'The things that helped, you can do again. If what you tried didn't help, then you may need to find something else to do . . . We will be finding out about a lot of ideas together and we will find something that works for everyone.

'Who can remember what else we talked about last time we met – about how worry might be good for us sometimes?' Remind children of the *fight, flight, freeze* response if they don't remember. 'In real danger, fighting, freezing or running away could save our life. This week we are going to talk about feelings we get in our body when we are anxious, frightened, or afraid.

'Imagine you are being chased by a tiger. How does your body feel?' (Prompt if necessary – racing heart, out of breath, sweaty hands, tummy ache, nausea.) 'Now think of a time you were worried or frightened. How did your body feel? Is it the same or different?' If it is a large group: 'Talk to a partner and see if your bodies felt the same way.' Have some children share.

'It's important for us to recognise these feelings so we know it means we are frightened. If the feelings are really strong, sometimes we can feel quite ill. Then we know we have to do something about it.'

Teaching activity

Show video

*(Note: Show **only the first half** of the book or video which looks at physical symptoms, Wilma Jean. The second half will be looked at in Session 8).*

'Does anyone get the same feelings in their body that Wilma Jean did? Which ones? Although not everyone's bodies react in exactly the same way, similar things are going on inside, making us ready to fight or flee.'

Share Body Template.

'We are each going to draw and write on this page how our own body feels when we are frightened or nervous.'

Discussion

'Sometimes we don't even know we are worried. We just feel ill. If we are feeling ill it is sometimes good to stop and think about whether we might be feeling sick because, really, we are worried. Our brains are trying to keep us safe by telling us there is something wrong and getting us ready to deal with it. A special part of our brain called the amygdala does this for us. It is our friend because it is trying to look after us, but sometimes it gets it wrong because it thinks we are in danger when we aren't.'

Distribute Mission sheet 2.3.

'Now we are going to write down on our mission sheet the ones that happen most often to us. We probably won't have all the same ones, because all our bodies are different.'

Conclusion

'Let's remember that word, the amygdala, because we will be talking about it in these sessions.'

Mission

'During this week your mission will be to notice if you feel any of these things and then stop to think if it means you are worrying about something. Tick any of the feelings you have in your body and note down if you think you were worried about something.'

Session 4. How can we help ourselves feel better?

Materials required

YouTube video (all ages) First half only of:

'Calm Down and Release the Amygdala'

https://www.youtube.com/watch?v=Zs559guIGDo

Worksheet 1.3 (Calming activities)

Mission sheet 2.4 (Practising a calming activity), one per student

Introduction/review

'Does everyone remember that we talked last week about how worry and anxiety make our bodies feel? Your mission was to think about your bodies and to notice when you felt any of these things. Did anyone notice any worry feelings in their bodies? What were the feelings in your body? What were the thoughts that went with them?' Allow discussion.

'We have talked about how everyone worries and that, when we are worrying, our brain (the amygdala) is trying to keep us safe. Sometimes the amygdala gets it wrong and so we feel worried when we don't need to be.'

Teaching activity

'Today we are going to try out some things to help us calm our bodies down when they don't need to fight or flee.'

Show video (watch the *first half only* of the video, the part that deals with the strategies. The second half of the video will be shown in a later session).

'All the things we have learnt today need to be practised. Once we get used to doing them, we can do them at any time we need to. But first we have to learn how to do them.'

Discussion/practice

'Let's start to practise these strategies now. First of all, square breathing.' Count the children through square breathing as shown on the video.

'How did that feel? Was it calming?'

'Now let's try another strategy on the video. Let's all be raw spaghetti . . . now cooked spaghetti! Let's practise with different parts of our bodies . . .

'Let's make our arms like raw spaghetti; now like cooked spaghetti.'

Repeat with other body parts, legs/neck/shoulders etc. 'How did that feel? Do you think you can relax your bodies like that – becoming cooked spaghetti – when you start to worry?

'Did anyone think of a safe place they would like to think about? Tell us about it. How does it make you feel to think about your safe place?' Not all children will be able to think of one, so don't force it.

Share and complete Worksheet 1.3.

Conclusion

'We have already shared ideas in previous group sessions about what we can do to make ourselves feel better. Today we have learnt three new strategies: square breathing, spaghetti bodies and the safe place. During the week I would like everyone to try one of these.'

Mission

'Draw or write on your mission sheet the strategy or strategies you are going to try this week: square breathing, spaghetti bodies, or safe place.

'I am really looking forward to hearing about how everyone gets on. Let's go round the group now, with everyone saying one thing that they enjoyed today.'

Session 5. Using our strengths to help us

Materials required

YouTube videos:

For younger children: 'Henry & Leslie (A Children's Story About Confidence and Self-Love)' https://www.youtube.com/watch?v=A2RIHM8xfmM

For older children and young people: 'Will.i.am. What I Am'

https://www.youtube.com/watch?v=cyVzjoj96vs

For all: 'Ish'. A story about not needing to be perfect https://www.youtube.com/watch?v=O6dTWLrAmTE

Worksheet 1.4 (Things I am good at)

Strengths Cards, by Jardine and Russell (2008), or develop your own list of strengths

Mission sheet 2.5 (Finding what we are good at), one per student

Review/introduction

'Last week we thought about different ways of helping ourselves when we are worried or nervous. Who tried out:

- Square breathing?
- Spaghetti relaxation?
- A safe place?

'How did it go?' Allow students to discuss.

'Today we are doing something new. We are all going to think of things we are good at – we call these our "strengths". We all have lots of things we are good at, but we don't always notice our strengths, so today we are going to think very hard at what we are good at and help each other notice things.

'Who can tell me something they are good at? Who can tell me something someone else in this room is good at?' Go round until everyone in the group has said a positive or been told a positive thing about themselves.

Teaching activity

Show video.

Discuss strengths that Henry and Leslie or Will have.

Share Strengths Cards or equivalent.

'Here are lots of good ideas for noticing strengths we might not have noticed we have. Let's each pick out two or three that are really like us.' Share.

'Now let's each think of one strength for someone in the group and tell them. This is called giving a compliment.' Ensure each child is complimented.

Discussion

'So now we realise we have strengths, how can these strengths help us?

Who can think of a way their strengths help them?' Go through the group so each student has at least one way their strengths can help.

Share Worksheet 1.4.

Conclusion

'Of course, we can have strengths in things without being perfect at them. Here is a video about being satisfied with what we can do.'

Watch video 'Ish'.

Mission

'Your mission this week is to find out more things you are good at. You can ask your family, friends or teachers and also think about it and notice when you do something well or well-ish. When you come back I want you to bring your mission sheets back with who you asked, what they said and some new strengths written on them.'

Session 6. Naming and taming emotions

Materials required

YouTube videos:

Younger children: 'Inside Out: Guessing the feelings'

https://www.youtube.com/watch?v=dOkyKyVFnSs

Older students: 'Identifying our feelings'

https://www.youtube.com/watch?v=VL5MvZKgVZA

For all: 'A Nifflenoo Called Nevermind'

https://www.youtube.com/watch?v=iN-Z8KRTXOc

Mission sheet 2.6 (Name that emotion), one per student

Review

'Who found out things they are good at, or good-ish at during the week? How did you find out? Did you work it out for yourself or did sometime tell you? Let's hear about some of them.' Encourage sharing.

'How did it make you feel to think about your strengths? Happy? Joyful? What is another word for feelings? Emotions! Are all emotions comfortable? No. Let's name some comfortable and some uncomfortable emotions. Sometimes we have a bad feeling, but we don't know the name of it. Then it's hard to deal with. When we know a name for what we are feeling it is easier to tell someone about it, and also to be able to manage it ourselves. Sometimes we call this "naming and taming" – like taming a wild animal. It is easier to tame something when we know what it is, so it helps us to know the exact name for the emotion we are feeling.'

Teaching activity

Younger children: 'Some of you have seen the film 'Inside Out' – it shows a cartoon of the sort of thing that goes on inside our head when emotions take over. We are going to watch some clips and I want you to guess the emotion.'

Show 'Inside Out' clips.

'What other emotion names do you know? Let's collect as many as we can and talk about what each one means and when we may have felt that way.'

Older students: 'We are going to watch a short video about emotions.'

Show video 'Identifying our feelings'.

Discuss.

Discussion

'We all have lots of emotions and they can change very quickly. Emotions are not good or bad; they are just there. But what do you think happens when emotions take over our actions? Sometimes our actions are not helpful if we let our emotions take charge. Sometimes, when we are too worried, we miss out on things we enjoy doing, like going to a party. Or we might miss doing a test we need to do, or homework we should be doing because we can't face it. Or we might worry about our homework so much that we do it all night and can't have any fun. It is helpful to notice our emotions and name them.'

Show video 'A Nifflenoo Called Nevermind'.

'Bottling up feelings can make them worse, so it helps to name your feelings and talk about them.'

Conclusion

'Can you remember a time when your emotions got the better of you? What happened? What could you do differently? Remember, we can use our strategies: breathing, spaghetti relaxation, safe place, applying our strengths.'

Mission

'Your mission for the week is to think hard about how you are feeling and write down at least three emotions you have, with the exact name and what was happening when you felt them.'

Session 7. Changing how we think

Materials required

YouTube videos:

'Calm Down and Release the Amygdala' (second half only)

https://www.youtube.com/watch?v=Zs559gulGDo

'Frozen, Think Positively'

https://www.youtube.com/watch?v=An2OalbPSII

Flip chart/white board/blackboard (optional)

Worksheet 1.5 (Red and green thoughts)

Mission sheet 2.7 (Red and green thoughts), one per student

Review/introduction

'Who noticed how they were feeling this week? Who can share what was happening and tell us what they called the emotion they felt?' Encourage sharing.

'Today we are going to learn about a way to change our thoughts. We are going to learn how to replace unhelpful (RED) thoughts with helpful (GREEN) thoughts.

'Who can remember what the amygdala is? It's that part of the brain that tries to take care of us, but sometimes overreacts. We need to help our amygdala calm down by reassuring it with helpful thoughts.'

Teaching activity

Show 'Calm Down and Release the Amygdala' second section, from four minutes in.

Discuss.

'Now we are going to watch a short clip from "Frozen". I want you to tell me what unhelpful (red) thoughts the snowman has at first. What could he have replaced them with?'

Show 'Frozen' clip.

Help students identify the snowman's red thoughts. Then help students find green thoughts to replace them. Record, if helpful, on whiteboard, flip chart or similar.

Discussion

'Who can think of some red thoughts they have had. How could you change that to a green thought?' Discuss and come up with options.

Distribute Worksheet 1.5 and ask students to write any red thoughts under the red picture and green alternatives under the green picture.

'Who came up with some really good green thoughts they could use to replace those unhelpful red thoughts? Can anyone think of any more green thoughts to replace the red ones?'

Allow students to share and help one another.

Conclusion

'Now we will finish with one green or helpful thought we have had today.' Give example: 'I can see that everyone in the group is learning.'

Go round and, if necessary, help all students to come up with a green thought.

Mission

'This week we are going to notice our thoughts and decide if they are helpful – green – or unhelpful – red – thoughts. If we come up with a red thought we will think hard about changing it to a green thought. During the week I want everyone to write down on their mission sheet at least one red thought they have and a green thought they can replace it with.'

Session 8. Doing things differently

Materials required

You Tube videos:

'Trouble in Paradise'

https://www.youtube.com/watch?v=am5lKJMibr0

'The Huge Bag of Worries' (book or video)

https://www.youtube.com/watch?v=G4obF25b6Fc&t=311s

Mission sheet 2.8 (Changing our actions), one per student

Review/introduction

'Last week/session we talked about changing our thoughts. Who noticed their red and green thoughts through the week? Who would like to share first?' Go through the mission sheets and have children discuss red thoughts shared, complimenting any children that changed red to green.

Ask students to come up with more green thoughts for red ones shared.

'This week we are talking about changing our behaviour/actions as well as our thoughts. Sometimes, when we have red thoughts they lead us into doing things that make our lives harder.'

Show video 'Trouble in Paradise'.

'What did Crab *think* when he saw the first coconut? Were those red thoughts or green thoughts? What did he *do?* How hard did he work to get rid of the coconut? Was that helpful? What happened next?'

Allow discussion.

'What could Crab have *done* differently? What are some green thoughts he could have had when he saw the coconut? How would they have changed his actions? What might his green actions have been?'

Teaching activity

Watch/read 'The Huge Bag of Worries'.

'What did the old lady do that helped Jenny act differently?'

Help students recognise that she *shared* her worries with a trusted person, *the friend sorted* her worries, Jenny *accepted* that some were typical and OK to have; some were *not her worries* and she *allowed someone else* to take care of some.

Discussion

'Is there anyone you could share your worries with? Does anyone here want to share any worries now?'

Allow discussion.

'How does it make us behave? What could we do differently?'

Help children recognise worries and find possible helpful green behaviours.

Conclusion

'When we think red thoughts we sometimes act in a red or unhelpful way. When we think green thoughts we act in a helpful, green way. The crab in "Trouble in Paradise" had lots of red thoughts about a harmless coconut and wasted all that time and energy getting rid of it . . . only to find another arrived right away. Sometimes we waste our energies in the same way.

'Now let's all say one thing we do that helps us.'

Mission

'Your mission for the week will be to choose one thing to do differently. Change your red action to green action. Note it down and be ready to share with us next week.'

Session 9. Choosing the strategies that work for us

Materials required

YouTube videos:

Younger children: 'Wilma Jean the Worry Machine' (book or video)

https://www.youtube.com/watch?v=gpAijfP99Ng (second half)

Older children and young people: 'Stress Management'

https://www.youtube.com/watch?v=hnpQrMqDoqE

or 'Stress Relief'

https://www.youtube.com/watch?v=UBupi8P2sRO

Worksheet 1.6, 1.7, 1.8 (Emergency first aid kit), according to choice, or create a design of your choice

Worksheet 1.9 (Review of strategies that work for you)

Mission sheet 2.9 (Using your emergency kit), one per student

Review/introduction

'Who managed to change a red action to a green action? How did that go?'

Discuss.

'Whilst we have been meeting, we have looked at a lot of different ways to help ourselves. The methods and plans we have made are called *strategies.* Some strategies work for some people and other strategies work for others. The trick is to choose the ones that might work for us and then practise them. That way we find what works best and can keep using those strategies. Next week will be our last session of this course (so sad! – I will miss meeting you all every week). This week I want us all to choose out the strategies that work for us.'

Teaching and discussion

Younger children:

'Do you remember Wilma Jean? She had a lot of worries and a lot of strategies. Let's look at what she tried.'

Watch second half of video from five minutes thirty-nine seconds or read second half of book.

'What did Wilma Jean's teacher suggest? What were her strategies?' Remind the children: lots of help from teacher and mother (for example, arriving early at party); separating worries into can/can't control; Worry Hat for worries she couldn't control.

Older children/young people:

Show 'Stress relief' or management video. Discuss the strategies outlined on the video.

'I have written down the strategies we have practised together.' Share Worksheet 1.9.

'Does anyone have any other strategies they would like to add? Do you want to add any from the video? Now you will be able to keep this list to remind you of everything we have learnt.'

Activity

'We have all been trying out these strategies and some will have worked better than others for each of us. Let's each of us pick the ones we want to use at the moment. Some of the other strategies might help us later.'

Share Worksheet 1.6, 1.7 or 1.8, or your own design, as appropriate.

'Now write or draw your favourite strategies in your emergency kit.'

Conclusion

'You have all done a great job of learning these new ideas. Next week we will review everything we have learnt together to help us all remember.'

Mission

'Choose one strategy from your kit to practise during the week.'

Session 10. Review and celebration

Materials required

YouTube video:

'Calm Down and Release the Amygdala'

https://www.youtube.com/watch?v=Zs559guIGDo

Party items – snacks, drinks, games

Certificates for each student

Review/introduction

'Who used their emergency kit last week? How did it go?

'We have covered such a lot in these weeks we have been together. So today I am going to show you a whole video that before we have just seen in parts. That should help remind us of all we have learnt. Who can remind us what the amygdala is?'

Teaching activity

Show video.

Discussion

'Now, let's think about the whole course and what we have learnt, including things we have seen on the video just now. What was most fun? What was most useful?' Record comments.

Certificates

'I am so proud of you all that I want to give you each a certificate for all the hard work you have put in and for how brave you have been. Now, remember to keep this certificate and your emergency kit somewhere you can find them, so when you need strategies in the future you can go to your kit. I will look forward to seeing how you are getting on, so be sure to keep using those strategies.'

Conclusion

'You have all worked very hard and helped each other try out new things. I have really enjoyed working with you and I will miss you a lot. I think you all deserve a bit of fun, so we will finish with a game/snack/little party.'

Summary

Introduction

Outline of ten-week programme

Session plans

1. Getting to know each other
2. What are worry and anxiety?
3. How does anxiety make us feel?
4. How can we help ourselves feel better?
5. Using our strengths to help
6. Naming and taming emotions
7. Changing how we think
8. Doing things differently
9. Choosing strategies that work for us
10. Review and celebration

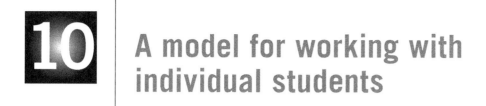

10 | A model for working with individual students

Introduction

Which youngsters benefit from this way of working?

The type of intervention offered in this chapter is most suited to generalised anxiety (Diagnostic and Statistical Manual of Mental Disorders, 2015). Whilst there may be helpful exercises for youngsters with obsessive/compulsive disorder (OCD) or who have post-traumatic stress disorder (PTSD), such issues are likely to require specialist intervention. Some areas of work, particularly around lifestyle changes, also require input from parents. Where this is lacking, the work may be compromised. It has also been the authors' experience that some children/young people are not ready to follow this type of programme and may benefit from alternative types of counselling and support; for example, person-centred counselling, acceptance and commitment therapy. It is always important to be guided by the child/young person and if you feel this approach is not suitable it may be necessary to refer the youngster for more specialist therapy or counselling. No-one should take on work beyond their skills and expertise, training or supervision.

CASE STUDY

Katya completed five sessions following the adapted cognitive-behavioural model as outlined in this chapter. It became increasingly clear that she was struggling to make sense of the activities and she explained that she did not feel comfortable. We therefore agreed with Katya and her parents to change our approach. We moved to a less structured, more person-centred approach in which Katya decided what she wished to focus on in sessions. For her, this was more successful.

Preparation

Working with individuals differs considerably from working with a group or class. Whilst there is the disadvantage that there are no others to share experiences and ideas, there is a great advantage in that the adult is able to follow the young person's lead, interests and pace. Individual work requires more knowledge and expertise than group work as the adult is constantly required to make judgements about the needs of the young person, which content areas to cover, which exercises to choose and the pace at which to work.

Chapter 6 covers important background arrangements, such as informed consent and supervision. If you do not regularly do individual work as a part of your role it is strongly advised that you review that chapter prior to commencing individual work with young people. Therapists and counsellors using this book will have their own theoretical backgrounds, methods and supervision arrangements already in place. They may, however, benefit from the resources recommended in this book, which they can use flexibly to support their work.

It is not possible to give set sessions for individual work as the adult will be led by the conversations that take place in the meetings, leading to the creation of tailored plans for each session. Therefore we are offering a framework for individual sessions which can be adapted by the adult, based on the age, interests, motivation and engagement of the child/young person. We are also offering a range of worksheets that may be used whenever particular issues arise or a specific area needs to be addressed. They are available to be photocopied in Appendix 3 and also online. Online resources can be personalised to match the interests of the individual. Language can be changed to match the child's preferences. For instance, whilst all individuals need to practise what has been learnt in a session in a real-life setting, you may wish to call this a 'task' with teenagers or a 'mission' with younger children. Case studies are provided within this chapter to illustrate some of our experiences of working with individuals.

An adapted cognitive-behavioural model

We have drawn on a range of models in this book, with cognitive-behavioural approaches featuring strongly. We know that behaviour, emotions and thoughts have complex interrelations. In our discussions with children and young people they have found it helpful to separate emotional from bodily feelings, and we have therefore addressed each area separately.

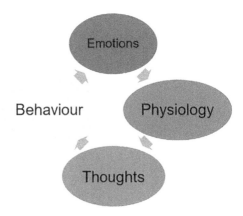

FIGURE 10.1 The adapted cognitive-behavioural model

Topics to cover

It is possible to take an individual child or young person through the structured sessions given in Chapter 9, and adults less experienced in individual work might welcome the structure that is offered. However, we have found that, when working with individuals, we soon find what their needs and preferences are, so we adapt the set structure and work more on their choices.

If you are not going to follow the same structure as the group work you will need to consider the topics you wish to cover in your planning. It is recommended that the following areas are covered over the course of the sessions, but it will necessarily be a more flexible approach than suggested for the group work:

1. Assessing, taking a baseline and consider setting goals (first session)
2. Understanding and expressing emotions
3. Identifying, challenging and changing negative thoughts
4. Challenging negative behaviours
5. Lifestyle changes
6. Relaxation
7. Reviewing progress, completing evaluations, including completing the original baseline measures again, deciding on any necessary further steps and celebrating progress (final session).

Each area may take several sessions to complete and it may be that in certain cases not all areas will be covered. All should, however, be considered and, where necessary, adapted. For instance, one of our young people was initially too anxious to recognise his own strengths. For this boy we looked out for individual strengths and successes and noted times when things were going well. These were then brought to his attention and we drew on them in helping him to make changes. You are likely to find that youngsters need more support in some areas than others. The benefit of working one-to-one is that you can depart from a structure to work more on the areas that the individual requires or responds to best.

In our work we have found it useful to have each session planned out in advance, even if we then depart from it according to the response we get. This ensures that any materials can be organised and that we can supply the structure for those who need it. However, we are not constrained by the plan if the session takes a different turn, so long as it is relevant to the work being done. Three suggested session plan frameworks are given below, one for an introductory session, one for a final session, and one which can be used for ongoing sessions. Introductory and final sessions have specific requirements which are captured in the frameworks given below. The 'ongoing' framework can be used repeatedly, and/or adapted, between the first and last sessions as the content will change depending on the previous session and the individual's responses in the session. The suggestions in the frameworks are necessarily incomplete as the adult will need to plan suitable activities adapted to the age and needs of the youngster. They will also need to keep notes of what happened in the session to help plan the next one. The resources provided in Appendix 3 can be drawn on to help teach individual points, following the youngster's interests and needs. This may change, week by week, so it is always a good idea to have a contingency plan. With young children we have often used a game as a closing activity to ensure a positive ending. With very young children it may be necessary to choose a game that is non-competitive or that you can be sure they will win.

When you meet the parents/carers to discuss informed consent it is useful to gain their views of the extent of the problem to form a baseline against which progress can be measured. It is also possible to ask the child or young person to complete their version of the questionnaire at this point. In certain circumstances it may be appropriate to ask school staff also to complete a baseline measure. If you are using a published measure, the RCAD scale (Chorpita et al, 2000) or the 'Strengths and difficulties questionnaire' (Goodman,1997) are available online, free of charge. An alternative structure for baseline measures is provided in Appendix 3.1, which can be adapted to suit your own circumstances in the e-resource version.

Framework for individual sessions

Session plan contents

The introductory session will necessarily differ from the others as it is 'testing the waters', getting to know the individual and setting the stage for the work.

Continuing sessions are the ones in which the bulk of the work is completed. This will cover these areas which interact with each other: emotions, thoughts, behaviour, lifestyle and relaxation. Each session will start with a review of previous work and any task set between sessions. This will provide valuable information about the pace and content of the current session. It may be that when you check in at the beginning of the session the young person presents you with an issue so severe that you need to deal with this before resuming the programme, or it may be that he or she is so anxious that you need to use more supportive exercises. Individuals may have areas they are more willing to address than others and their preferences can be followed. You will need to use your judgement to decide which to address and when.

The final session is an important one as it reviews the strategies which have been most useful and will most likely stay in the mind. It may be difficult to end the work, as a positive relationship should have been built and the child or young person must not be left feeling deserted or abandoned. If it is considered that he or she would benefit from further work, how and with whom should be discussed in this session. Suitable services and professionals should be identified.

Introductory session

This involves assessing, taking a baseline and discussing aims for the intervention.

The main aims of this session are:

- To establish rapport
- To give the young person a 'taster' of the type of activities you are offering, so he or she can make an informed decision on whether to continue to take part
- To assess the motivation to change
- To take a baseline if this has not yet been completed
- To begin to identify strengths
- To discuss aims for the intervention.

Establishing rapport is essential for successful work, as the quality of the relationship between the individual and the adult is key. It is likely that the young person will have little idea of what the sessions will be like, so it is helpful to explain not only the sort of exercises that will take place but also the atmosphere, ground rules and confidentiality agreement with the necessary exceptions.

Exercises based on finding the young person's strengths are helpful here for building confidence that the sessions will be run sensitively and respectfully, and that challenges will be within the control of the individual and not beyond their ability.

Exercises around how satisfied the young person is with how things are at the moment, what they would like to change and how much work they are willing to put in gives the adult an indication of what will be acceptable to them. If a baseline was not completed in advance of the sessions beginning, this can be taken now. Aims and, if appropriate, goals for the intervention can then be discussed.

At the end of the session the individual should be given the opportunity to decide whether to commit to a series of sessions now that they have experienced one. The individual must feel that he or she has a genuine choice and is not feeling pressured by parents or intimidated by the "counselling" environment.

After the session you will need to evaluate how it went, how the young person responded and the issues they shared. Ideally you will then be able to discuss this with your supervisor and use it for planning your next session. An exemplar for this session is given at the end of this chapter.

CASE STUDY

Alice's parents described her as 'very anxious and depressed' and requested our support. In the first session Alice denied feeling either anxious or depressed but conceded that she was 'stressed' and she wished to be 'less stressed'. She was offered a choice of activities for the session which included a relaxation exercise, a behaviour change exercise or a cognitive 'thinking' exercise. She didn't wish to address either thoughts or behaviours but was willing to try a relaxation exercise. Square breathing was taught which she found 'very calming'. At the end of the session Alice was clear she wanted more sessions and specified that they should include more relaxation exercises. Only much later in the intervention, when trust had been built, was she able to speak more openly about her anxiety and high levels of distress.

Ongoing sessions

1. Understanding and expressing emotions

   All ongoing sessions will start with a check-in to assess how the young person is feeling, whether they did any between-session tasks and what they feel able to do at this stage.

   Naming emotions is a very helpful stage in managing them. Not all young people will be able to recognise or name their emotions, and if this is the case then work is required. They may interpret bodily responses as physical sickness when they are actually stress responses. As emphasised elsewhere, the possibility of there being an actual physical cause should be excluded before treating the symptoms as emotional.

   Once a young person is able to recognise and name emotions, which may include finding a whole range of specific words and phrases for different types and levels of anxiety, they will be better placed to express them appropriately.

CASE STUDY

George was a very bright boy who had an exceptional talent for thinking through his difficulties in detail. He could not understand why his rational thought processes were not helping him to reduce his anxiety. After some sessions it became clear that George was not finding it easy to consider the role that his emotions were playing on his thoughts and behaviours. There was one occasion on which he was very disappointed with his own performance. When we discussed this, he was trying to resolve the issue by telling himself it did not matter and he could try to do it again. However, he found that this did not help with his feelings of depression and anxiety. We discussed the importance of acknowledging his feelings of disappointment, accepting the strength of his emotions and giving them some attention before he moved on from them. By naming and acknowledging his disappointment he was able to accept it without it exacerbating his anxiety and depression.

2. Identifying, challenging and changing negative thoughts

All sessions require an introductory activity to 'check-in' with the individual, find out how they are feeling and how resilient or vulnerable they are feeling at the time. You may need to alter your plan if they appear very fragile and you had planned to challenge their perceptions.

Identifying, challenging and changing negative thoughts is an important concept in cognitive-behavioural approaches, which assume that many unpleasant emotions come from an overly negative interpretation of experiences, leading to unhelpful thoughts and hence behaviours. You will need to provide an appropriate level of challenge to the youngster whilst being sensitive to how much they are ready to manage at this stage. In our experience, some relish a challenge early on in the process whilst others find it too hard and prefer to start with a different area, such as relaxation. You may therefore want to change and/or provide the exercises in later sessions.

3. Identifying, challenging and changing negative behaviours

Once the prerequisite of changing thoughts has taken place it will then be easier to concentrate on changing behaviour. Young people need help to understand how the two link. They may need to look first at other people through stories and videos before they can apply this to themselves. For example, in Aesop's fable of the ant and the grasshopper, the ant's behaviour (to work hard and store food for winter) was based on a correct belief that winter was coming. The grasshopper's mistaken belief that summer would never end led to his behaviour of having fun and not working. Accurate thinking leads to suitable behaviours.

CASE STUDY

Grace was very keen to attend a weekend youth camp, but highly anxious about it as she had become very distressed at a previous camp. Her recurring thoughts had been 'I want to go home' and 'This is never going to end'. This led to Grace calling her parents and going home (the behaviour) for a break in the middle. We brainstormed helpful thoughts from which she chose her top 10 and wrote them down to take with her. They included 'I'll see my mum on Sunday' and 'I had so much fun last time that by the end I didn't want to go home'. Grace successfully attended camp for the full weekend and, as a result, her confidence soared.

4. Lifestyle changes

As described in Chapter 8, there are many ways that lifestyle affects our mental and physical health. From discussion with the young person, and sometimes a parent, you will find out if there are areas of their lifestyle that may be exacerbating the anxiety. Nutrition, hydration, diet, exercise and screen time can all be explored. Depending on their age, some lifestyle choices may be out of their control, in which case liaison with the parents is beneficial. However, with teenagers the aim will be to provide explanations (including any research findings) about why they should consider making changes. If an individual is not motivated to change, this may be all you can do at this stage, leaving him or her with the information they need. Equally, parents may need a high level of motivation to assist their children in making life-style changes which will affect the family.

CASE STUDY

Zane, aged 9, had developed a number of unhelpful lifestyle habits, includ-ing lack of exercise and over-eating, which led to his being overweight. His parents, who were also overweight, requested that we work on helping him change these habits and lose weight. However, his parents wanted him to eat healthy food whilst they continued their high-fat diet and they wanted him to take exercise in the garden on his own whilst they remained indoors. Zane himself did not feel he was overweight and had no motivation to exercise, pre-ferring to play games on his tablet. We considered that asking a 9-year-old to change his behaviour without parental support and modelling was unrealistic and asked his parents to return when they felt able to change their own eating and exercise habits.

CASE STUDY

Benazir took little exercise as she was too anxious to attend most social events and rarely left the house. She did not enjoy sports and had no motivation to exercise. Eventually, after brainstorming a wide range of exercise options, she reluctantly asked to go for walks in the evening with her father. She found to her surprise that she enjoyed the walks, which had the additional benefit of individual conversation with her father, which was otherwise rare in her large family. These walks became a regular part of family life.

5. Relaxation

These sessions are about finding ways to help the body and mind relax, to reduce sensitivity to anxiety (turn down the 'worry alarm') and find peace and calm. Whilst choosing a healthy lifestyle can help here, we have found that many students respond very well to relaxation methods. They can also be used in sessions that young people are finding very difficult to finish positively.

CASE STUDY

Jeri had been badly bullied in and out of school and could not bear to think about it. She rejected several of the exercises offered as they reminded her of her experiences but enjoyed the relaxation exercises. In one session we practised the visualisation and she described it as 'awesome'. We therefore got parental permission to record the visualisation on to her phone so that it was continuously available to her. She used it to help her fall asleep, thus also addressing a key lifestyle issue that had been troubling her.

Final session – review, evaluation and celebration

Before the final session it is helpful to ask parents and young people (and school staff, if appropriate) to complete once more the measure used as a baseline. This feeds into the evaluation of work. The final session should be a review of work undertaken, celebration of progress made and a plan for any further support required. We have found that youngsters value the sessions greatly and we do not want them to feel abandoned when they finish. This is one reason for negotiating in advance the expected number of sessions, although this can be renegotiated as the intervention progresses.

We have also found it helpful if the young person creates their own form of 'aide memoire' of any strategies or helpful ideas they have accumulated throughout the sessions.

These help maintain change. If it is possible to organise a follow-up session after an interval, this is also likely to motivate the child or young person to keep using the new skills as well as feeling supported over time.

If more work is needed this is the time we can set that up, whilst being careful not to break any confidences (unless required for safety).

CASE STUDY

Faye was a teenage girl who responded well to the intervention sessions. She built up a good relationship with the adult and felt emotionally safe. Endings were difficult for Faye both within the individual sessions and at the end of the agreed number of sessions. She often remembered something very important that had happened during the week just as a session was about to end. It was important to be strict about the boundaries within the structure so that she realised that the adult was in control of the session, which is important for emotional safety. We offered follow-up meetings prearranged on a regular basis (once a half-term) so that she could be reminded of strategies, apply them to new situations and feel supported over time. This helped her accept the end of the weekly sessions.

Session plan exemplars

Introductory session

Resources
Worksheet 3.1.1 (Baseline measures)
Worksheet 3.1.2 (What went well this week)
Optional: Strengths Cards, age-appropriate game

Purpose	Plan
Build rapport, establish ground-rules.	Introduce self. Ask what would make him/her comfortable. Suggest some ground-rules: • Honesty • Confidentiality (limited by my need to keep him/her safe) • Giving choices • Open to trying things out (not all will work) • Explain that it will be their choice to continue for six sessions if they feel comfortable.
Baseline measures to assess motivation to change.	Complete Appendix/Worksheet 3.1.1 (Baseline measures)

Build confidence, rapport, make a positive beginning.	Ask them for their story. Ask them when they began to feel anxious, for times they feel less anxious (people, places, times, situations). Notice and reflect strengths and successes.
Find out how things are going at the moment.	Ask them to describe how they are at this moment and, if appropriate, score how they are feeling from 1–10.
Young person to set their own aims for the intervention.	Ask what are the most important things to change and which they would like to work on first?
Trial an activity based on the young person's information so far.	Ask them to tell you what they are good at. If they find this difficult, ask them what others would say they were good at (parents, friends, teachers). Optional – use Strengths Cards or list of strengths.
If suitable, set a task so that practice can take place in a real-life session.	Ask them to keep a diary for a week if they are happy to, looking out for things going well. Give Worksheet 3.1.2.
Gain informed consent from youngster.	Ask them if they wish to continue.
Complete the session with the young person feeling comfortable.	Reflect back positives from the session. With a young child it may be helpful to finish with a suitable game.
After the session Assess their current needs. Assess the session, evaluate which approaches seemed valuable for this individual. Consider suitable ways forward in the light of this session.	Evaluation/Reflection Discuss session with supervisor. Note issues arising in the session and note which exercises seem to appeal to/help the most. Recognise individual strengths and identify areas for development. Plan next session.

ongoing session (one of a number of sessions on relaxation)

Resources Worksheet 3.6.1 Worksheet 1.3 Worksheet 2.4	
Purpose	Plan
Review last session, how the week has gone, and the task if one was agreed.	Ask them how their week has been and how they are feeling now. If appropriate, give a rate from 1–10. Remind them of the content of the last session. Ask how they found the task (if set).
Trial two more relaxation exercises.	Explain which exercises you are going to trial and how and why they might help. Practise them together. Discuss whether either or both helped them relax.

Arrange to practice in real-life setting.	Choose task according to preference. (If neither felt comfortable move on to another topic; i.e., emotions, thoughts and behaviours, lifestyle).
Finish session with the young person feeling comfortable.	Reflect back positives from the session.
	If age appropriate, play a short game suited to the youngster's age and preference. Notice any particular strengths.
After the session	Evaluation/Reflection
Assess their current needs.	Discuss session with supervisor.
Assess the session, evaluate which approaches seemed valuable for this individual.	Note issues arising in the session and note which exercises seem to appeal to/help the most. Recognise the strengths of the young person and identify areas for development.
Consider suitable ways forward in the light of this session.	Plan next session.

Final session

Resources
Worksheets 1.6, 1.7, 1.8 (choose most appropriate)
Worksheet 3.7.1
Optional – celebration materials: snack, drink, game

Purpose	Plan
Review last session, how the week has gone, task if one was agreed.	Ask them how their week has been and how they are feeling now. If appropriate, give a rate from 1–10. Ask how they found the task (if set). Remind them of the work covered during the intervention.
Return to the baseline measure initially used.	If this was given out between sessions, it can be reviewed. Otherwise complete within session.
Create a long-lasting aide-memoire to help maintain use of strategies.	Complete chosen worksheet(s) together.
Make plan for the future	Discuss what information from the sessions can be shared with others. Come to mutual agreement. (This may include other professionals, especially if you choose to refer/signpost on.) Agree if there will be any follow-up meetings.
Create a positive ending to the intervention and build confidence for the future.	Compliment the young person on all progress made and strengths noticed. If appropriate, celebrate with a treat – game, biscuits, drink.

Resources

Resources for individual work can be found in Appendix 3. They can be photocopied as they are, or the e-versions can be personalised. There are also websites of videos to demonstrate the concepts in each of these areas in the group work sessions described in Chapter 9.

Summary

Introduction

Preparation

An adapted cognitive-behavioural model

Topics to cover

Session plan contents

➤ Introductory session
➤ Ongoing sessions
➤ Ending session

Session plan exemplars

Resources

Appendix 1
Group session worksheets (Chapter 9)

Worksheet 1.1

Worry words

Here are a lot of words people use to talk about feeling worried. There are spaces at the bottom to add any other words you use.

Afraid	Aghast	Antsy	Anxious
Apprehensive	Basket-case	Bugged	Butterflies
Choked	Concerned	Disquieted	Distressed
Disturbed	Dreading	Fidgety	Fretful
Hyper	In a state	In a tizzy	In pieces
In suspense	Jittery	Jumpy	Nervous
Nervy	Overwrought	Restless	Scared
Shaken up	Shaking	Shivery	Spooked
Strung out	Taut	Troubled	Uneasy
Uptight	Watchful	Wired	Worried sick

Worksheet 1.2

My fear thermometer

Worksheet 1.3

Calming strategies

Think about your safe place and draw it in the cloud

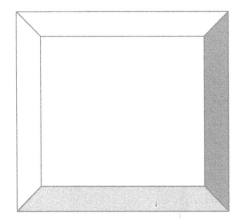

Practise your square breathing

In, 2, 3, 4

Hold, 2, 3, 4

Out, 2, 3, 4

Hold, 2, 3, 4

Turn your raw spaghetti body into cooked spaghetti!

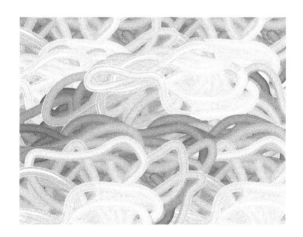

Tick the strategy you like the best:

Thinking of your safe place

Square breathing

Spaghetti bodies

Worksheet 1.4

Strengths

1 I am good at ....

   This could help me when I am worried because ....

   ....

2 I am good at ....

   This could help me when I am worried because ....

   ....

3 I am good at ....

   This could help me when I am worried because ....

   ....

Worksheet 1.5

Red and green thoughts

RED

GREEN

Worksheet 1.6

My Emergency Back Pack

Take this wherever you go. (Think of Dora the Explorer!)

©Elizabeth Herrick and Barbara Redman-White

Emergency Tool Box.

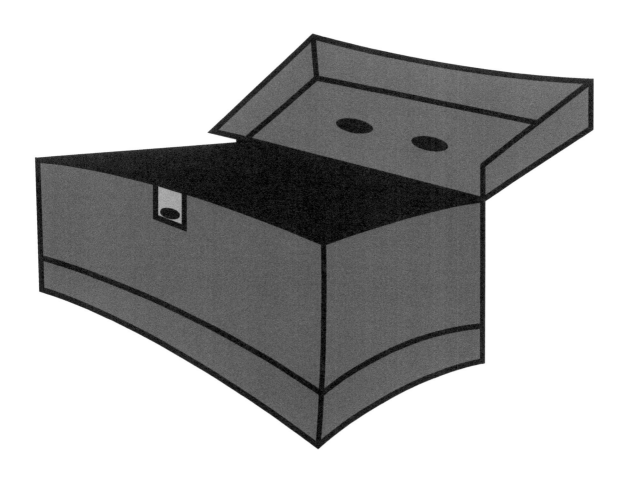

The tools I have chosen to help me are:

....

....

....

....

Name .... Date ....

My Emergency Velvet Pouch.

The Magic Spells that will help me are

....

....

....

....

Name .... Date ....

Worksheet 1.9

We have talked about things that help us to feel good, choose 3 for your emergency backpack.

Review strategies that work for you.

Choose some for your emergency kit.

Go outside and enjoy nature

Take some exercise

Talk to somebody

Draw how you feel

Drink water

Write about how you feel

Square breathing

Look at your Fear Thermometer

Tell yourself it is just your worry alarm and not a real danger

Play your snakes and ladders game, go up some ladders

Do something you are good at

Change your Red thoughts to Green thoughts

What else works for you?

Appendix 2
Group session tasks (Chapter 9)

Mission 2.1 – Smiling

Name .... Date ....

Your mission this week is to smile at everyone from your group – every time you see them. Other people would like it if you smiled at them too!

In the table say what happened:

WHO DID I SMILE AT?	DID THEY SMILE BACK?

Mission 2.2 – Trying out an idea

Name .... Date ....

Your mission this week is to try out something new to help when you are feeling worried.

Complete this sentence to say what you will do.

This week, when I feel worried or frightened, I will

....

....

....

....

....

DRAW YOURSELF DOING IT

Mission 2.3 – Noticing how our bodies feel

Name _____ Date _____

Your mission this week is to notice when you have any of the feelings below.

Then decide if they were because you were worried about something.

Now write what you think in the second column.

FEELING IN YOUR BODY	WHAT MIGHT I BE WORRYING ABOUT?

Mission 2.4 – **Something calming to practise**

Name .... Date ....

Your mission this week is to try out one of the ideas you have heard about today

- square breathing
- cooked spaghetti
- thinking about a safe place.

Now finish the following sentence to say what you will do.

This week if I feel worried or frightened. I will ....

....

....

....

....

....

DRAW YOURSELF DOING IT

Mission 2.5 – What are your strengths?

Name .... Date ....

Your mission this week is to:

ask people about what they think your strengths are and to think about what you think you do well or well-ish.

WHO DID I ASK?	WHAT DID THEY SAY?

I think I do these things well or well-ish:

....

....

....

....

Mission 2.6 – Name that emotion

Name .... Date ....

Your mission this week is to think about how you have felt during the week.

Can you give a name to those emotions?

Have you tried to talk to someone about them?

WHAT EMOTION DID I FEEL?	DID I TELL ANYONE ABOUT THIS?	WHO DID I TALK TO?

Mission 2.7 – Changing red thoughts to green

Name .... Date ....

Your mission this week is to notice at least one red thought and change it into a green one.

Write or draw your thoughts in the table below.

If you come up with more you can, of course, put those in too!

RED THOUGHT	GREEN THOUGHT

Mission 2.8 – Changing our actions

Name .... Date ....

Your mission this week is to make one helpful change from red action into green action.

An example is given to you in the table below.

WHAT I USED TO DO (RED ACTION)	WHAT I DID INSTEAD (GREEN ACTION)
Example of red action I used to hide in the library at break time.	Example of green action I asked my friend if she would help me and we went out to break together.
My Red Action	**My Green Action**

Mission 2.9 – Using your emergency kit

Name .... Date ....

Your mission this week is to practise one of the strategies you have chosen to put in your toolkit.

Complete the following sentence.

This week I will practise: ....

....

....

....

....

....

DRAW YOURSELF DOING IT

Appendix 3

Worksheets for working with individuals (Chapter 10)

Worksheet 3.1.1

Baseline measures Children

Name ....

Rate each of the following on a 1–10 scale, putting a cross where you feel you are right now. 1 = not very much, 10 = as much as it could be.

How badly is anxiety affecting your life?

1—-2—--3--—4--—5----6--—7—--8—--9—--10

What would be a good enough score for you to get on with your life?

1—-2—--3--—4--—5----6--—7—--8—--9—--10

What is your worst anxiety? ....

Where is it on the scale?

1—-2—--3--—4--—5----6--—7—--8—--9—--10

What would be a good enough score for you to get on better?

1—-2—--3--—4--—5----6--—7—--8—--9—--10

Is there another anxiety you would like to tackle? ....

....

If so, where are you on the scale with that?

1—-2—--3--—4--—5----6--—7—--8—--9—--10

Where would be a good enough place to be with this issue?

1—-2—--3--—4--—5----6--—7—--8—--9—--10

Worksheet 3.1.2

What went well this week?

Date ....

Keep a note of what has gone well this week. You can draw it or write a few words.

	MORNING	AFTERNOON	EVENING
MONDAY			
TUESDAY			
WEDNESDAY			
THURSDAY			
FRIDAY			
SATURDAY			
SUNDAY			

Worksheet 3.2.1

Things that make me feel good

Worksheet 3.2.2

Emotions word search

See if you can find the following emotions in this word search

CHEERFUL	BORED	PROUD
SAD	ANGRY	EXCITED
HAPPY	GUILTY	UPSET
HURT	SCARED	LONELY

C	D	E	R	A	C	S	U	T	A	O	F	R	C	N
X	Q	S	E	M	V	J	S	T	U	P	S	E	T	P
X	K	D	K	T	P	S	A	E	J	T	X	V	R	J
J	G	E	O	S	R	A	X	G	H	T	Z	L	T	I
B	M	R	W	Q	E	D	U	O	R	P	S	H	R	O
L	D	O	P	H	F	L	U	N	G	X	B	R	U	H
V	B	B	K	C	G	L	V	B	Y	P	P	A	H	A
M	D	W	T	U	S	L	Z	F	O	R	G	S	B	Y
V	P	D	I	S	R	R	U	S	P	H	G	X	Y	B
A	F	L	Z	C	A	L	M	F	V	W	W	N	L	X
V	T	M	U	B	K	P	S	A	R	O	B	G	A	K
Y	M	K	L	O	N	E	L	Y	V	E	T	R	H	D
D	F	J	F	C	M	M	X	C	R	V	E	C	H	D
E	X	C	I	T	E	D	G	N	D	Z	S	H	D	B
V	X	Y	A	M	L	X	M	I	Y	K	H	J	C	A

Worksheet 3.3.1

Thinking patterns

Identifying alternative ways of thinking can be useful in helping to shift moods and feelings.

Thoughts that make me feel anxious:

....

....

....

....

Thoughts that make me feel good:

....

....

....

Worksheet 3.3.2

My support network

Draw your support network in the circles below.

Start with yourself in the centre.

Build outwards with people and services that are available and important to you:

- family, such as ....
- extended family, such as ....
- friends, such as ....
- people in the community, such as ....
- services and institutions, such a ....

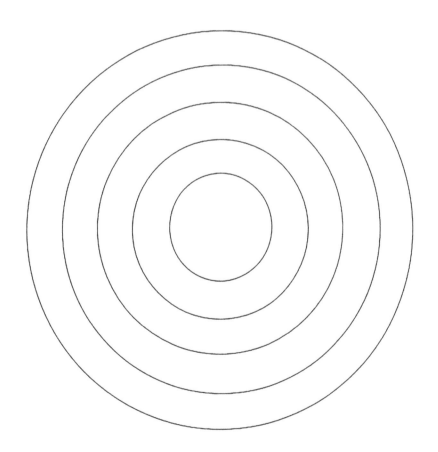

Worksheet 3.4.1

S.M.A.R.T targets

When we are changing our behaviours it can be difficult to know where to start. We need to set goals we can achieve fairly easily to start with. If your goal is Specific, Measurable, Achievable, Relevant and Time-based you are more likely to be successful. Try filling in the following areas to help you.

The issue I want to work on is

....

....

Specific: What I want to be able to do is

....

....

....

Measurable: I will know I have achieved it when

....

....

....

Attainable: I believe this is possible YES/NO

Relevant: I believe this will help me achieve my long-term goals   YES/NO

Time-based: I want to have achieved this by

....

I am going to celebrate when I make it by

....

....

Worksheet 3.5.1

Well-being

All of the things below are things people have found help them stay calm. Circle the ones that work for you and add anything else.

1. Being in nature

    Walking

    Fresh air

    Playing/helping in the garden

    Other ....

2. Taking exercise

    Running

    Walking

    Dancing

    Sports

    Other ....

3. Being creative

Painting

Drawing

Writing a journal

Writing stories

Sewing/knitting

Making/mending things

Drama

Other ....

4. Being with animals

Having a pet

Visiting a person with a pet

Walking a dog

Other ....

5. What else works for you?

....

....

....

....

Worksheet 3.5.2

The five senses

Sometimes, when we are anxious, we worry so much that we lose touch with what is really happening. It can be helpful to 'ground' ourselves by focusing on the reality around us.

At a time when you are calm, think about what you enjoy with your five senses.

You might choose to put together a box with lovely things in to concentrate on when you are beginning to get anxious.

I like to see/look at ....

....

I like to eat/taste ....

....

I like to smell ....

....

I like to listen to/hear ....

....

I like to touch ....

....

Worksheet 3.5.3

Sleep hygiene

If you are having difficulty sleeping, check the following:

➤ Avoid stimulating drinks before bed; e.g. drinks with caffeine.

➤ Try to relax in the hour before bedtime.

➤ Keep your bedroom for calm, quiet activities, games.

➤ Keep technology out of your bedroom.

➤ If you need to keep technology in your room, avoid using it when you are in bed.

➤ Maintain a cool temperature in your bedroom.

➤ Ensure you are comfortable in bed; i.e. mattress, pillow, warmth, sleep wear.

➤ Remove or reduce distracting noises and lights as far as possible.

➤ Try to have your evening meal at least two hours before going to bed.

➤ Go to bed and get up at approximately the same time every day, including weekends.

If you have followed all this advice and you are still having trouble sleeping, you may need to see your doctor.

Visualisation

> Relaxing can be difficult sometimes. The following exercise is a guided relaxation script which can help children and teens to relieve stress and anxiety.
>
> The script can be read to a child or young person and/or it can be recorded so that it can be played back whenever it is needed.
>
> Sit or lie in a comfortable position. *If you wish, you can play relaxing music.*

Gently close your eyes and slowly breathe in and out through your nose. (PAUSE) Take in a deep breath and slowly let it out. (PAUSE) Take in another deep breath and slowly breathe out. (PAUSE)

Imagine you are walking in a garden on a pleasantly warm day. (PAUSE) On a bench sits a friendly looking woman in brightly coloured, strange-looking clothes. She is sewing and has a basket of brightly coloured materials by her side. (PAUSE) She tells you that this is the garden of tranquility. (PAUSE) While you are there you can leave all your worries with her and she will stitch them into a quilt. (PAUSE) You leave all your worries with her and walk on. (PAUSE)

There is lush, green grass with flowers scattered everywhere. (PAUSE) You lie down on it. (PAUSE) You look up into the beautiful blue sky. (PAUSE) You see white fluffy clouds like cotton tufts. (PAUSE) You watch as a big, soft cloud gently drifts towards you. (PAUSE) See it float gently down to the ground. Climb on to the cloud. (PAUSE) Feel how soft and comfortable it is. As you

Worksheet 3.6.1 Continued

breathe, feel the softness of the cloud. (PAUSE) You notice that the cloud is turning pink. As you breathe in, you fill your lungs with the lovely soft, calm pink of the cloud. (PAUSE) Enjoy the calm feeling. (PAUSE) Think of your favourite colour. As you think of it, the cloud slowly changes to that colour. (PAUSE) Take a deep breath and breathe in your favourite colour. Breathe in and out slowly. (PAUSE) Change the colour of the cloud. Notice how that colour feels. (PAUSE) Change the colour one more time. Notice how that colour feels. (PAUSE) Now, as you breathe out, watch all the colours flow out of the cloud like a rainbow.

(PAUSE) Say to yourself, 'I am relaxed. I feel good. The colours are pretty and relaxing.' (PAUSE) Take another breath and blow the rainbow cloud away. Watch it drift back up into the sky. (PAUSE) You are back lying on the lush grass. (PAUSE)

You get up and walk back the way you came. (PAUSE) You meet the sewing lady who has sewn all your worries into a slightly odd, brightly coloured quilt. (PAUSE) She lets you choose whether you want to take it with you or leave it with her. (PAUSE) You walk back out of the tranquil garden. (PAUSE)

When you are ready, wiggle your fingers and toes. Open your eyes and stretch. Notice how relaxed and good you feel.

This has been adapted from:

50 Activities for Teaching Emotional Intelligence. Level 1 Elementary' Publ. PRO-ED 1996, Introduction and Theory by Dianne Schilling and also

Go-Zen.

Many more relaxation scripts can be found on YouTube.

©Elizabeth Herrick and Barbara Redman-White

Breathing exercises

Try all of these and see which work for you.

Brief breathing exercises:

Imagine you are an enormous balloon filled with air and let the air out of your mouth very slowly, making a quiet 'sssssss' sound.

Take in a big breath of air through your nose and then blow it out gently through your mouth on to your hand. See how long you can make your out-breath last – time it if you like.

Blow bubbles! A long slow out-breath will make the biggest bubbles.

Breathe in deeply, as if you were smelling a lovely flower, and then blow out slowly, as if you were making a candle flame flicker but not blowing it out.

Breathe in deeply through your nose, raising your shoulders and then drop your shoulders sharply whilst blowing breath out of your mouth.

Sustained breathing exercises:

The yogic 'square' or 'box' breathing. Breathe in through the nose for a slow count of three, hold the breath for a count of three, breathe out through the mouth for a count of three. Hold the non-breath for a count of three; repeat. The count can increase with practice but the count should be the same for all parts of the exercise, hence 'square'.

Counting down from 100 with each breath. Silently say '100' with the in-breath through the nose, then breathe out slowly through the mouth. Then silently say '99' with the next in-breath, then breathe out slowly through the mouth, then '98' etc. Inevitably you will lose count at some point, so just go back to 100 and start again until feeling calm.

Worksheet 3.7.1

Aide memoire

NEVER WORRY ALONE
• Talk with someone you trust

GET THE FACTS
• Your worry may be rooted in wrong or incomplete information.

MAKE A PLAN
• You will worry less when you feel more in control.

Review your strategy sheet.

✓ How is your body feeling, can you make it feel better?

✓ Are you noticing your emotions and allowing yourself to feel them without judging them?

✓ Are you having negative thoughts? Can you change them? If not, let them pass. They will not be there for ever.

✓ Be your own best friend – be kind and self-compassionate, as if you were talking to someone else.

Appendix 4

PowerPoint and information sheets for parent workshops

Appendix 4.1

Parent Workshop
Powerpoint Presentation

PARENT WORKSHOP

AN INTRODUCTION TO UNDERSTANDING ANXIETY IN CHILDREN AND YOUNG PEOPLE

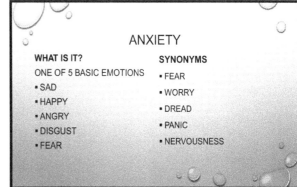

ANXIETY

WHAT IS IT?
ONE OF 5 BASIC EMOTIONS
- SAD
- HAPPY
- ANGRY
- DISGUST
- FEAR

SYNONYMS
- FEAR
- WORRY
- DREAD
- PANIC
- NERVOUSNESS

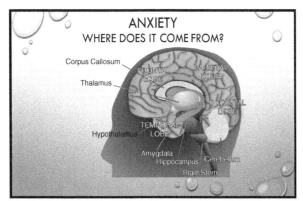

ANXIETY
WHERE DOES IT COME FROM?

Corpus Callosum, Thalamus, FRONTAL LOBE, PARIETAL LOBE, OCCIPITAL LOBE, TEMPORAL LOBE, Hypothalamus, Amygdala, Hippocampus, Cerebellum, Brain Stem

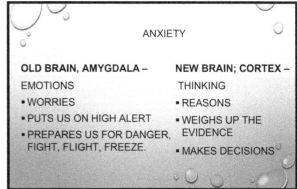

ANXIETY

OLD BRAIN, AMYGDALA –
EMOTIONS
- WORRIES
- PUTS US ON HIGH ALERT
- PREPARES US FOR DANGER, FIGHT, FLIGHT, FREEZE.

NEW BRAIN; CORTEX –
THINKING
- REASONS
- WEIGHS UP THE EVIDENCE
- MAKES DECISIONS

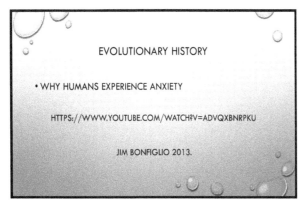

EVOLUTIONARY HISTORY

- WHY HUMANS EXPERIENCE ANXIETY

HTTPS://WWW.YOUTUBE.COM/WATCH?V=ADVQXBNRPKU

JIM BONFIGLIO 2013.

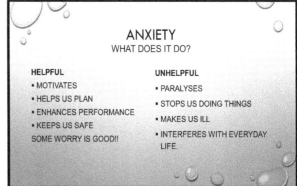

ANXIETY
WHAT DOES IT DO?

HELPFUL
- MOTIVATES
- HELPS US PLAN
- ENHANCES PERFORMANCE
- KEEPS US SAFE
SOME WORRY IS GOOD!!

UNHELPFUL
- PARALYSES
- STOPS US DOING THINGS
- MAKES US ILL
- INTERFERES WITH EVERYDAY LIFE.

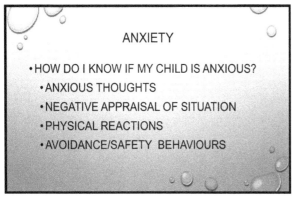

ANXIETY

- HOW DO I KNOW IF MY CHILD IS ANXIOUS?
- ANXIOUS THOUGHTS
- NEGATIVE APPRAISAL OF SITUATION
- PHYSICAL REACTIONS
- AVOIDANCE/SAFETY BEHAVIOURS

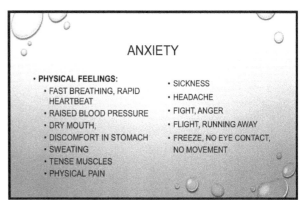

ANXIETY

- PHYSICAL FEELINGS:
  - FAST BREATHING, RAPID HEARTBEAT
  - RAISED BLOOD PRESSURE
  - DRY MOUTH,
  - DISCOMFORT IN STOMACH
  - SWEATING
  - TENSE MUSCLES
  - PHYSICAL PAIN
- SICKNESS
- HEADACHE
- FIGHT, ANGER
- FLIGHT, RUNNING AWAY
- FREEZE, NO EYE CONTACT, NO MOVEMENT

Appendix 4.1 Continued

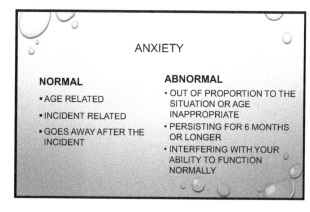

ANXIETY

NORMAL
- AGE RELATED
- INCIDENT RELATED
- GOES AWAY AFTER THE INCIDENT

ABNORMAL
- OUT OF PROPORTION TO THE SITUATION OR AGE INAPPROPRIATE
- PERSISTING FOR 6 MONTHS OR LONGER
- INTERFERING WITH YOUR ABILITY TO FUNCTION NORMALLY

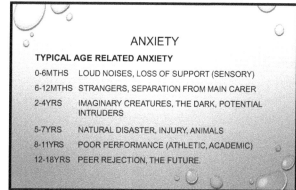

ANXIETY

TYPICAL AGE RELATED ANXIETY

0-6MTHS	LOUD NOISES, LOSS OF SUPPORT (SENSORY)
6-12MTHS	STRANGERS, SEPARATION FROM MAIN CARER
2-4YRS	IMAGINARY CREATURES, THE DARK, POTENTIAL INTRUDERS
5-7YRS	NATURAL DISASTER, INJURY, ANIMALS
8-11YRS	POOR PERFORMANCE (ATHLETIC, ACADEMIC)
12-18YRS	PEER REJECTION, THE FUTURE.

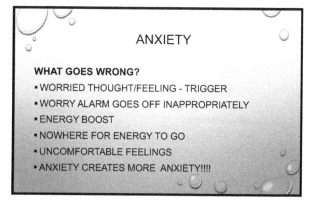

ANXIETY

WHAT GOES WRONG?
- WORRIED THOUGHT/FEELING - TRIGGER
- WORRY ALARM GOES OFF INAPPROPRIATELY
- ENERGY BOOST
- NOWHERE FOR ENERGY TO GO
- UNCOMFORTABLE FEELINGS
- ANXIETY CREATES MORE ANXIETY!!!!

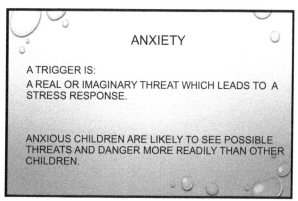

ANXIETY

A TRIGGER IS:
A REAL OR IMAGINARY THREAT WHICH LEADS TO A STRESS RESPONSE.

ANXIOUS CHILDREN ARE LIKELY TO SEE POSSIBLE THREATS AND DANGER MORE READILY THAN OTHER CHILDREN.

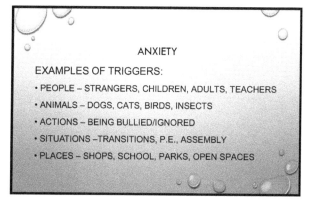

ANXIETY

EXAMPLES OF TRIGGERS:
- PEOPLE – STRANGERS, CHILDREN, ADULTS, TEACHERS
- ANIMALS – DOGS, CATS, BIRDS, INSECTS
- ACTIONS – BEING BULLIED/IGNORED
- SITUATIONS –TRANSITIONS, P.E., ASSEMBLY
- PLACES – SHOPS, SCHOOL, PARKS, OPEN SPACES

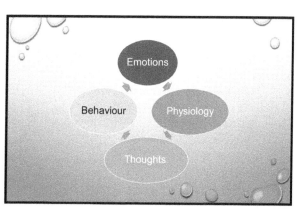

Emotions

Behaviour

Physiology

Thoughts

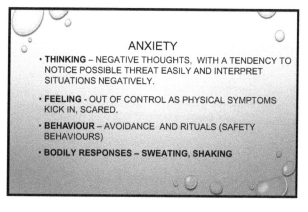

ANXIETY
- **THINKING** – NEGATIVE THOUGHTS, WITH A TENDENCY TO NOTICE POSSIBLE THREAT EASILY AND INTERPRET SITUATIONS NEGATIVELY.
- **FEELING** - OUT OF CONTROL AS PHYSICAL SYMPTOMS KICK IN, SCARED.
- **BEHAVIOUR** – AVOIDANCE AND RITUALS (SAFETY BEHAVIOURS)
- **BODILY RESPONSES** – SWEATING, SHAKING

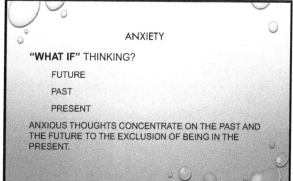

ANXIETY

"WHAT IF" THINKING?

FUTURE

PAST

PRESENT

ANXIOUS THOUGHTS CONCENTRATE ON THE PAST AND THE FUTURE TO THE EXCLUSION OF BEING IN THE PRESENT.

©Elizabeth Herrick and Barbara Redman-White

Appendix 4.1 Continued

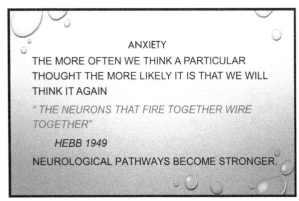

ANXIETY

THE MORE OFTEN WE THINK A PARTICULAR THOUGHT THE MORE LIKELY IT IS THAT WE WILL THINK IT AGAIN

"THE NEURONS THAT FIRE TOGETHER WIRE TOGETHER"

HEBB 1949

NEUROLOGICAL PATHWAYS BECOME STRONGER.

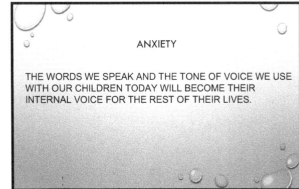

ANXIETY

THE WORDS WE SPEAK AND THE TONE OF VOICE WE USE WITH OUR CHILDREN TODAY WILL BECOME THEIR INTERNAL VOICE FOR THE REST OF THEIR LIVES.

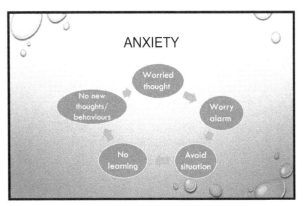

ANXIETY

Worried thought → Worry alarm → Avoid situation → No learning → No new thoughts/behaviours

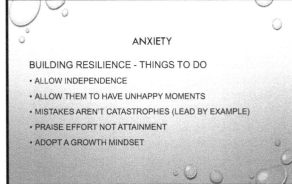

ANXIETY

BUILDING RESILIENCE - THINGS TO DO

- ALLOW INDEPENDENCE
- ALLOW THEM TO HAVE UNHAPPY MOMENTS
- MISTAKES AREN'T CATASTROPHES (LEAD BY EXAMPLE)
- PRAISE EFFORT NOT ATTAINMENT
- ADOPT A GROWTH MINDSET

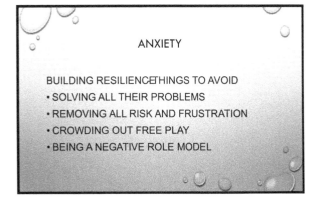

ANXIETY

BUILDING RESILIENCE–THINGS TO AVOID

- SOLVING ALL THEIR PROBLEMS
- REMOVING ALL RISK AND FRUSTRATION
- CROWDING OUT FREE PLAY
- BEING A NEGATIVE ROLE MODEL

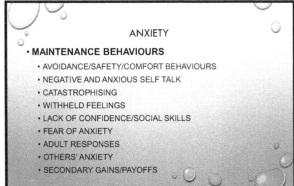

ANXIETY

- **MAINTENANCE BEHAVIOURS**
  - AVOIDANCE/SAFETY/COMFORT BEHAVIOURS
  - NEGATIVE AND ANXIOUS SELF TALK
  - CATASTROPHISING
  - WITHHELD FEELINGS
  - LACK OF CONFIDENCE/SOCIAL SKILLS
  - FEAR OF ANXIETY
  - ADULT RESPONSES
  - OTHERS' ANXIETY
  - SECONDARY GAINS/PAYOFFS

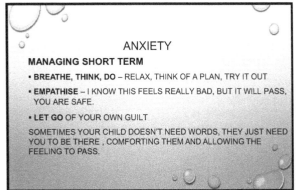

ANXIETY

MANAGING SHORT TERM

- **BREATHE, THINK, DO** – RELAX, THINK OF A PLAN, TRY IT OUT
- **EMPATHISE** – I KNOW THIS FEELS REALLY BAD, BUT IT WILL PASS, YOU ARE SAFE.
- **LET GO** OF YOUR OWN GUILT

SOMETIMES YOUR CHILD DOESN'T NEED WORDS, THEY JUST NEED YOU TO BE THERE , COMFORTING THEM AND ALLOWING THE FEELING TO PASS.

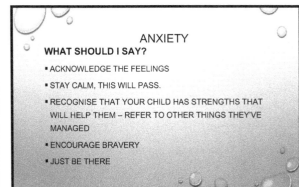

ANXIETY

WHAT SHOULD I SAY?

- ACKNOWLEDGE THE FEELINGS
- STAY CALM, THIS WILL PASS.
- RECOGNISE THAT YOUR CHILD HAS STRENGTHS THAT WILL HELP THEM – REFER TO OTHER THINGS THEY'VE MANAGED
- ENCOURAGE BRAVERY
- JUST BE THERE

Appendix 4.1 Continued

ANXIETY
WHAT SHOULD I NOT SAY?
- IT IS GOING TO BE OK, TRUST ME
- THERE'S NOTHING TO BE SCARED OF
- LET ME TELL YOU ALL THE REASONS YOU DON'T HAVE TO WORRY
- STOP BEING SUCH A WORRIER
- I DON'T UNDERSTAND WHY YOU ARE SO WORRIED
- DON'T BE SILLY/CHILDISH
- YOU ARE OLD ENOUGH TO MANAGE THIS NOW

(49 PHRASES TO CALM AN ANXIOUS CHILD WWW.GOZEN.COM)

ANXIETY
WHAT SHOULD I DO?
- IDENTIFY EARLY SIGNS AND SIGNALS
- CREATE AND USE AN EMERGENCY TOOL BOX FOR DIFFICULT MOMENTS
- WAIT UNTIL YOUR CHILD IS CALM BEFORE DISCUSSING THE DIFFICULTIES
- DEVISE A PLAN WITH YOUR CHILD TO HELP THEM TO FACE THEIR FEARS
- KEEP YOURSELF EMOTIONALLY HEALTHY
- BE A GOOD ROLE MODEL

ANXIETY

TRY THESE 'QUICK FIXES' 1
- GO OUTSIDE
- DO SOMETHING CREATIVE
- WRITE/DRAW HOW YOU FEEL
- DRINK WATER

ANXIETY

TRY THESE 'QUICK FIXES' 2
- TAKE A DEEP BREATH
- LISTEN TO SOOTHING MUSIC
- FIND A DISTRACTION
- TAKE EXERCISE

ANXIETY

MYTHS
- YOU SHOULD BE ABLE TO CONTROL YOUR CHILD'S ANXIETY
- CHILDREN MUST CHANGE THEIR NEGATIVE EMOTIONS
- YOUR CHILD SHOULD BE ANXIETY FREE

ANXIETY

FURTHER SUPPORT
- SUPPORT GROUPS
- REFERENCES FOR PARENTS
- USEFUL WEBSITES

ANXIETY

IF YOU HAVE FOUND THIS PRESENTATION USEFUL YOU MAY CONSIDER PURCHASING:

" SUPPORTING CHILDREN AND YOUNG PEOPLE WITH ANXIETY: A PRACTICAL GUIDE."

ELIZABETH HERRICK AND BARBARA REDMAN-WHITE

(ROUTLEDGE 2018)

DISCUSSION AND QUESTIONS

Appendix 4.2

Factors that help to maintain anxiety

Below are some of the types of behaviours that can unwittingly maintain or support anxiety. It is important to be aware of them, so we can change them.

Avoidance behaviours

Avoidance of the situation that is feared; for example, going to school on the days that involve changing for PE. If we avoid situations that we are anxious about we do not learn that the situation may not be as difficult as we thought it would be, or that we can develop coping strategies to help us deal with difficult situations. Instead we learn that we feel better if the situation is avoided, as the fear goes away temporarily. This leads to more anxiety on the next occasion. Every time the situation is avoided it becomes less likely that we will manage it the next time.

Safety behaviours

These behaviours give a false sense of security. Some children develop habits or rituals which can later be hard to break. These may be physical actions (sometimes self-injurious), excessive checking, rituals and obsessions; for example, if I drink three glasses of water before I go to bed I will not have nightmares.

Comfort behaviours

Comfort behaviours help us to feel better and are likely to replace an emotional expression of feelings. These may be helping to divert attention from, and provide relief for, difficult and painful feelings. They also provide a sense of control when other things feel chaotic. Over- or under-eating can be comfort behaviours.

Negative, anxious self-talk

Telling yourself everything will go wrong; for example, 'If I go to the party no-one will want to talk to me. I will be on my own and feel lonely and miserable.' These thoughts lead to avoidance behaviours.

Appendix 4.2 Continued

Catastrophising

This involves thinking that one mistake or difficulty will end in disaster; for example, 'I always get everything wrong, I am no good at anything. I will never pass any exams, my life has been ruined.'

Mistaken beliefs

These are assumptions about ourselves, others and life in general. We tend to take them for granted, not realise they are beliefs, but assume they reflect reality; for example:

- Life is a struggle,
- I can't cope with difficult situations,
- I should always pretend I am OK, no matter how I feel.

Withheld feelings

If we cannot recognise our feelings it is very difficult to address them. It is important to discuss how things feel even when the feelings are hard to manage. If we pay attention to our feelings they will settle, feel less frightening and be under our control. If we ignore them they will build up and 'leak out' in our thoughts and behaviours when we are not expecting it. This makes our behaviour look erratic and leads to feeling out of control, which may be in itself quite frightening.

Lack of confidence/poor social skills

It is not uncommon for children with anxiety to have weak social skills, which can lead to poor relationships with peers and adults. Friendships are very important for children as they are growing up and we know how essential it is for teenagers to feel that they belong to their group of friends. Limited social skills can lead to a lack of confidence, which can stop someone feeling that they can try out new situations. Children who do not pick up social skills naturally can be taught them directly.

Appendix 4.2 Continued

Fear of becoming anxious

Anxiety feeds on itself. Even when we are not anxious about something specific we may become anxious about becoming anxious. This means that our body is on high alert; i.e., the worry alarm is on most of the time, which can be exhausting and interfere with our ability to learn from our mistakes, develop confidence and resilience and enjoy everyday activities.

Unhelpful adult responses

Overprotection of children and young people does not help them experience new things and develop skills and resilience for coping with the difficulties that will arise from time to time. If we allow children/young people to avoid a difficult situation we are reinforcing their feeling that it is a scary situation and that they do not have the resources to cope with it effectively.

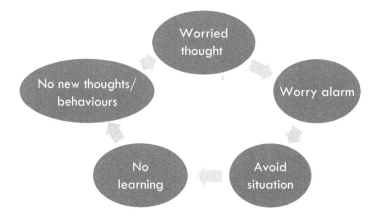

FIGURE 1.1 Over-protection cycle

Giving in to your child's anxiety will make it worse in the long run. This is a tough message and it is obviously easier to say than do. Children are very good at pressing our emotional 'buttons' and making us feel guilty and upset if we do not give in to their demands; for example, 'I am ill, I need to stay off school', or 'I will be sick if you make me go to the dentist'. However, unless we begin to help children and young people learn better ways to manage their anxieties they will not learn that the world is not such a scary place and that they do have the resources to cope.

Appendix 4.2 Continued

Catching anxiety

Anxiety is easily 'caught' from adults (and vice versa), so it can affect children and young people when there are other anxious people in the home environment or the classroom. We are programmed to notice and respond to other people's emotions, which can lead to us feeling the same emotions that those close to us are feeling. Emotions are easily transferred from one person to another.

Secondary gains/payoffs

It is possible that children or young people are being reinforced in their anxiety behaviours by getting a 'better deal' (in their eyes) when they express anxiety. For example, they may get more adult attention, extra treats or special treatment. It is important that we do not inadvertently reinforce our children's behaviours by providing more positive attention when they are anxious and ignore them when they are not. Shifting our attention focus to the behaviours that are healthy is very helpful.

Appendix 4.3

Practical tips for parents

This information sheet gives a wide range of strategies that children and young people have found useful. Select some that you think may work for your family and try them out.

Teach your child that anxiety is normal, explain how it works. Explain that some worry is good, discuss with your child when it is helpful that you have a worry alarm which can be set off to warn you of danger. Explain that our worry alarm sometimes gets too bossy and interferes with our thinking brain.

Allow them to worry

- have a specific worry time
- have a worry hat/bag/box
- perhaps allow them to pick out only one at a time
- write different stories with alternative endings.

Use 'What is' rather than 'What if' – think about the now rather than the future or the past.

Tell them that thoughts come and go like a train; let them come, watch them as they pass, wave goodbye. They are just thoughts, thoughts cannot harm us.

Identify your child's 'superpowers' (strengths). How can they help us solve a problem?

Identify what relaxes your child (and you!). When are you most calm? Write a list of three of the people, places, things that make you feel calm.

Help your child to find a way of expressing their worry:

Can you draw it?

If how you feel was a monster, what would it look like?

If you gave your feeling a colour, what would it be?

Appendix 4.3 Continued

Distraction techniques

I need you to tell me when two minutes have gone by

Let's count . . . (anything relevant)

I will say something and I want you to repeat it.

Develop an emergency checklist – things to do when the worry alarm has been set off. Personalise it with your child:

Breathing

Calming activity identified earlier

Creative visualisation – soothing, happy place

Take exercise

Pretend to blow up a balloon.

Read a therapeutic story together; for example, *Teenie Weenie in a Too Big World*, by Margot Sunderland and Nicky Armstrong (Speechmark), or *What to Do When You WORRY Too Much*, by Dawn Huebner (Magination Press).

Say: 'This feeling will go away. Let's get comfortable until it does.'

Remember, we are role models for our children – learn together.

Appendix 4.4

Relaxation and calming

Try to recognise the early signs and signals of your child's anxieties and intervene as soon as possible. The earlier you intervene the easier it will be for you to calm your child. Below is a selection of strategies.

Breathing techniques

Imagine you are blowing up an enormous balloon filled with air. Picture letting the air out as slowly as you can, until the balloon goes flat.

Play a game, notice your breath, see how long it takes you to breathe out. See who can breathe out the slowest, making a 'sssssss' sound, like a snake.

Lie on the floor, put hands on the tummy and feel the tummy expand on the in-breath and relax on the out-breath. If this is difficult, put something light on the tummy – a cuddy toy, or a cushion – and see if the child can make the object go up and down with the breathing. Demonstrate if necessary.

Breathe in deeply, as if you were smelling a lovely flower, and then blow out slowly, as if you were making a candle flame flicker but not blowing it out.

Breathe in deeply through the nose, raising your shoulders and then drop your shoulders sharply whilst blowing the breath out of the mouth.

Imagine you have a pot of bubble liquid. Take in a deep breath. Slowly and gently blow bubbles around the room. The bubbles may have colours or pictures in them.

Relaxation

Imagine you are a piece of spaghetti. Make your body into an uncooked piece of spaghetti, tall, straight, arms and legs squeezed into your body. Squeeze your whole body as tight as you can for ten seconds. Then let your body go and relax. Now imagine you are a cooked piece of spaghetti, floppy, soft and flexible.

Lie down on the floor and imagine you are ice cream melting in the summer sun. Enjoy the feeling as you relax your body.

Pretend to be a rag doll, see who can be the floppiest.

Appendix 4.4 Continued

Sit or lie as still as you can. Tell each part of your body to relax, one part at a time. Feet, legs, tummy, chest, arms, neck, face. Give yourself time before you get up and do other things.

Exercise

Jump up and down or shake your body as fast as you can for as long as possible. Now, stop and feel your body fizzing like lemonade.

Do some physical exercise, trampolining, running, walking, dancing, sport. This may also get you out into nature, which is known to be relaxing and calming.

Staying in the present

Recognise what is happening now rather than worrying about what happened in the past or what might happen in the future.

Think of three things you can see

three things you can taste

three things you can smell

three things you can hear

three things you can touch.

Apps to support calming

Breathe, Think, Do, Sesame: app for younger children.

Stop, Breathe and Think Kids: free app for older children.

Headspace: for young people.

Appendix 4.5

Separation anxiety

If your child is having difficulties separating from you at school it will be important to work closely with the school to devise an appropriate plan for supporting your child. Consistency between home and school will make it easier for the child to feel safe and secure. If it becomes so intense that the child is refusing to come to school, or feeling ill to avoid attending, encourage them to get back to school as soon as possible. The longer a child is away from school the more difficult it will be for him or her to attend comfortably.

There is a lot that parents and teachers can do to help make the child feel safer.

- Stay patient and calm.

- Set firm limits and apply them consistently.

- Develop a clear routine for the morning prior to coming to school and keep it consistent.

- Develop a goodbye ritual. This may include taking a cuddly toy from home or something of yours that is comforting. This will remind the child of you and of home and provide reassurance that you are coming back to collect them.

- Offer two appropriate choices, so that your child has some level of control; for example, 'Would you like one hug and two kisses before I leave you at school today or two hugs and one kiss?', or 'Would you like to keep my scarf with you at school today or your teddy from home?'

- Leave without fuss, tell your child you are leaving and that you will be back and then leave without hesitating or stalling.

- Find out if there is an adult or a 'buddy' your child can stay with when they get to school.

- Try not to give in and make sure you have a support network or a distraction to help you recover from any distress.

- Praise your child for any small improvements.

- Make sure you have special individual time at home together at the end of the day.

For further information and guidance, see Chapters 7 and 8.

Appendix 4.6

How to manage panic attacks

If it is possible that this is a serious medical event and not a panic attack, medical help should be summoned. Panic attacks are not dangerous, although they can be frightening. A child who has repeated panic attacks may be able to take part with parents (and, if appropriate, school staff) in agreeing a suitable plan which is likely to include the following elements.

Do

- If possible, take your child somewhere quiet

- Stay with them until the panic attack has subsided

- Let the panic run its course, as trying to stop it may fuel it

- Stay calm and reassuring, speak slowly and calmly

- Remind the child that he or she is safe and that this will pass

- Encourage the child to breathe, concentrating on slowing the breathing down

- Hold, cuddle, or stroke your child

- Return to normal activities once your child is calm and, if needed, rested.

Do not

- Tell children to calm down

- Get cross or tell them they are naughty, difficult, just being a nuisance

- Tell them to grow up

- Tell them there is nothing to worry about

- Try to discuss what the problem is.

For further information and guidance, see Chapter 7.

Appendix 4.7

Parents as role models

We know that children learn from watching others and are particularly affected by those close to them. As parents we are therefore acting as role models for our children and young people.

Ask yourself the following questions:

- Do you find it difficult to talk about and express your feelings?

- Do you consider the world to be a threatening place at times?

- Do you have times when you can't think clearly and rationally (fight or flight mode)?

- Do you suffer from any of the physical effects of anxiety and worry?

- Do you find yourself thinking negative and catastrophic thoughts?

- Do you avoid situations you are worried about?

If you are answering yes to several of these questions, you may want to think about how you are managing your own anxiety whilst supporting your child with theirs.

We have to help ourselves first – think of the oxygen mask on a plane.

Try to:

- Identify your own stress levels

- Notice when you are anxious – physical symptoms

- Accept that your emotions are real and valid

- Practise positive self-talk

- Take time for yourself

- Be a friend to yourself

- Be 'good enough', no-one is perfect

- Seek help if you need it.

Appendix 4.8

References and websites for parents

Books for adults:

Collins-Donnelly, K. (2014) *Starving the Anxiety Gremlin.* Jessica Kingsley Publishing

Guarino, R. (2015) Me and My Feelings: What Emotions Are and How We Can Manage Them. Hoopoe Books

Plummer, D.M. (2010) Helping Children to Cope with Change, Stress and Anxiety. Jessica Kingsley Publishing

Stallard, P. (2002) *Think Good-Feel Good.* John Wiley and Sons

Books for children:

Huebner, D. (2006) *What to Do When You Worry Too Much.* Magination Press

Huebner, D. (2007) What to Do When Your Brain Gets Stuck. Magination Press

Ironside, V. (2011) *The Huge Bag of Worries.* Hodder Children's Books

Sunderland, M. & Armstrong, N. (2000), *A Nifflenoo Called Never Mind.* Speechmark

Sunderland, M. & Armstrong, N. (2000), *Willy and The Wobbly House.* Speechmark

Sunderland, M. & Armstrong, N. (2003), *Teenie Weenie in a Too Big World.* Speechmark

Websites:

www.youngminds.org.uk – national charity, providing support and advice for parents and young people. Helpline available

www.gozen.com – downloadable resources, videos and webinars

www.parentzone.org.uk – online discussion between parents for advice and support

www.YouTube.com – Dr. Pooky Knightsmith, video clips and webinars

Apps for children:

Breathe, Think, Do, Sesame: app for younger children

Stop, Breathe and Think Kids: free app for older children

Headspace: for young people

Bibliography

American Psychiatric Association (2013) *Diagnostic and Statistical Manual of Mental Disorders* (5th edn, updated 2015). Arlington, VA: American Psychiatric Publishing

Bagwell, C.L. et al. (1998) 'Preadolescent friendship and peer rejection as predictors of adult adjustment.' *Child Development*, 69, 140–153

Barlow, D.H. (2002) *Anxiety and its Disorders* (2nd edn). New York: Guilford Press

Baumeister, R. (2005) 'Rejected and alone.' *Psychologist* 18(12), 732–735

Beck, A.T. & Emery, G. (1985) *Anxiety Disorders and Phobias: A Cognitive Perspective.* Cambridge, MA: Basic Books

Blumenthal, J.A., Smith, P.J. & Hoffman, B.M. (2012) 'Is exercise a viable treatment for depression?' *ACSM's Health & Fitness Journal*, 16(4), 14–21

Bowlby, J. (1978) *Attachment and Loss.* Harmondsworth: Penguin

Bowlby, J. & Ainsworth, M. (1992) 'The origins of attachment theory.' *Developmental Psychology*, 28, 759–775

Brotheridge, C. (2017) *The Anxiety Solution.* UK: Penguin Random House

Cannon, W.B. (1929) *Bodily Changes in Pain, Hunger, Fear and Rage.* New York: Appleton Century-Crofts

Charlie Waller Memorial Trust (2016) 'Mental health and well-being policies for schools & colleges. Example policy & guidance: Raising awareness and fighting depression.' Available at: www.ghll.org.uk/mental-health-policy-and-guidance-for-schools

Chorpita, B.F. et al. (2000) 'Assessment of symptoms of DSM-IV anxiety and depression in children: A revised child anxiety and depression scale.' *Journal of Behaviour Research and Therapy*, 38, 835–855

Collins-Donnelly, K. (2014) *Starving the Anxiety Gremlin.* London: Jessica Kingsley Publishers

Cooper, P. & Cefai, C. (2009) 'Contemporary values and social context: Implications for the emotional wellbeing of children.' *Emotional and Behavioural Difficulties*, 14(2), 91–100

Cross, D. & Lester, L. (2014) *Pastoral care: A 10-step plan.* Online publication

Day, L. (2016) 'Resilience for the digital world.' Young Minds and Ecorys. Available at: www.youngminds.org.uk

De Shazer, S. et al. (2007) *More Than Miracles: The State of the Art of Solution Focused Brief Therapy.* New York: Routledge

Department for Education (2015) *Supporting Pupils With Medical Conditions at School.* London: Department for Children, Schools and Families

Department for Education (2015) *Special Educational Needs and Disability. Code of Practice: 0 to 25 Years. Statutory guidance for organisations which work with and support children and young people who have special educational needs or disabilities.* London: Crown Copyright

Devon, N. (2018) *A Beginner's Guide to Being Mental: An A to Z.* London: Bluebird

Duty of Care (2017). Available at: www.education.vic.gov.au

Dweck, C.S. (2017) *Mindset: Changing the Way You Think to Fulfil Your Potential.* CreateSpace, independent publishing platform

Eley, T.C. et al. (2007*)* 'A twin study of panic.' *Journal of Child Psychology and Psychiatry*, 48, 1184–1191

Eley, T.C. et al. (2008) 'In the face of uncertainty: A twin study of ambiguous information, anxiety and depression in children.' *Journal of Abnormal Child Psychology*, 36, 55–65

Equality Act (2010). Available at: www.legislation.gov.uk

Faupel, A. (2003) *Emotional Literacy: Assessment and Intervention. Ages 7–11.* London: nferNelson

Faupel, A. (2003) *Emotional Literacy: Assessment and Intervention. Ages 11–16.* London: nferNelson

Faupel, A., Herrick, E. & Sharp, P. (2017) *Anger Management: A Practical Guide for Teachers* (3rd edn). London: Routledge

Foley, A.E., Herts, J.B., Guerriero, S., Levine, S.C. & Beilock, S.L. (2017) 'The math-anxiety performance link. A global phenomenon.' *Current Directions in Psychological Science*, 26, 52–58

Fox, C. & Boulton, M. (2006) 'Friendship as a moderator of the relationship between social skills problems and peer victimisation.' *Aggressive Behavior,* 32, 110–121

Freeman, D. & Freeman, J. (2012) *Anxiety: A Very Short Introduction.* UK: Oxford University Press

Gerull, F.C. & Rapee, R.M. (2002) 'Mother knows best: Effects of maternal modelling on the acquisition of fear and avoidance behaviour in toddlers.' *Behaviour Research and Therapy,* 40, 279–287

Goleman, D. (1996) *Emotional Intelligence: Why It Can Matter More Than IQ.* London: Bloomsbury

Goodman. R. (1997) 'Strengths and difficulties questionnaire.' *Journal of Child Psychology and Psychiatry,* 38(5), 581–586. Available at: www.sdqinfo.com

Greenland, S.K. (2016) *Mindful Games.* Boulder, CO: Shambhala Publications

Guarino, R. (2015) *Me and My Feelings: What Emotions Are and How to Manage Them.* Los Altos, CA: Hoopoe Books

Hanson, R. (2013), *Hardwiring Happiness: The Practical Science of Reshaping Your Brain and Your Life.* London: Ebury Publishing

Harris, R. (2013). Available at: www.actmindfully.com.au

Hart, A. & Taylor, S. (2011) *Mental Health Toolkit and the Resilience Therapy Toolkit.* Available from: Mind Brighton and Hove, 57 New England Street, Brighton. Tel: 01273 666950

Hart, D. (2003) *Teachers' Thinking in Environmental Education.* New York: Peter Lang

Hartup, W. (1994) 'Having friends, making friends and keeping friends.' *Emergency Librarian*, 94, 21, (3) 30–32

Hayes, S.C. et al. (2012) *Acceptance and Commitment Therapy: The Process and Practice of Mindfulness Change* (2nd edn). New York: Guilford Press

Hebb, D.B. (1949) *The Organization of Behaviour.* New York: Wiley

HMI Series: Curriculum Matters No.14 (1989) 'Personal and social education from 5 to 16.' London: Her Majesty's Stationery Office

Hudson, J.L. & Rapee, R.M. (2009*)* 'Familial and social environments in the etiology and maintenance of anxiety disorders,' in M.M. Antony & M.B. Stein (eds.) *Oxford Handbook of Anxiety and Related Disorders.* New York: Oxford University Press

Jardine, K. & Deal, R. (2008) Strength Cards. Available from: www.amazon.co.uk

Karst, P. (2001) *The Invisible String.* Camarillo, CA: De Vorss & Co

Le Doux, J. (1998) *The Emotional Brain.* New York: Phoenix

Learning Through Landscapes (2003). Available at: www.ltl.org.uk/childhood/learning.php

Luxmoore, N. (2000) *Listening to Young People in School, Youth Work and Counselling.* London: Jessica Kingsley Publishers

Maslow, A.H. (1943) 'A theory of human motivation.' *Psychological Review, 50(4)*

Maslow, A.H. (1968) *Towards a Psychology of Being.* New York: Van Nostrand

Micco, J.A. (2017) *The Worry Book for Teens.* Oakland, CA: Instant Help Books, New Harbinger Publications

Miller W.R. & Rollnick S. (2002) *Motivational Interviewing: Preparing People to Change.* New York: Guilford Press

Moore, M. & Carr A. (2000) 'Anxiety disorder,' in A. Carr (ed.) *What Works With Children and Adolescents.* London: Routledge

Mosley, J. (1996) *Quality Circle Time in the Primary Classroom.* UK: LDA

Nadge, A.J. (2005) 'Academic care: Building resilience, building futures.' *Journal for Pastoral Care and Personal-Social Education,* 23(1), 28–33

National Commission on Education (1996) *Success Against the Odds: Effective Schools in Disadvantaged Areas.* London: Routledge

Pennebaker, J.W. (2004) *Writing to Heal.* Oakland CA, New Harbinger Press

Potter, M. (2014) *How Are You Feeling Today?* UK: Featherstone Education

Prochaska, J. & DiClemente, C.C. (1983) 'Stages and processes of self-change. Toward an integrative model of change.' *Journal of Counselling and Clinical Psychology,* 51, 390–395

PSHE Association (2017) *Guidance for Teaching About Mental Health and Well-Being.* Available at: https://www.pshe-association.org.uk

Reynolds, P. (2005) *Ish.* London: Walker Books

Riuz, F.J. (2012) 'Acceptance and commitment therapy versus traditional cognitive behaviour therapy: A systematic review and meta-analysis of current empirical evidence.' *International Journal of Psychology and Psychological Therapy* 12(3), 333–358

Rock, D. (2009) *Your Brain at Work.* New York: HarperCollins

Rudd, P., Reed, F. & Smith, P. (2008) *The Effects of the School Environment on Young People's Attitudes Towards Education and Learning.* NfER: www.nfer.ac.uk

Rusakas, F. (2008) *I Love You All Day Long.* New York: HarperCollins

Russell, L. (2018) *Mental Health in the Digital Age.* Parentzone: www.parentzone.org.uk/event/mental-health-digital-age

Rutter M. et al. (1979) *15000 Hours.* Cambridge, MA: Harvard University Press

Scaife, J. (2008) *Supervision in Clinical Practice. A Practitioner's Guide.* London: Routledge

Seden, J. (2018). Open University, www.open.ac.uk

Selman, R.L. & Jaquette, D. (1977) 'Stability and oscillation in interpersonal awareness,' in C.B. Keasey (ed.) *The Nebraska Symposium on Motivation.* Lincoln, NE: University of Nebraska

Sharp, P. & Herrick, E. (2000) 'Promoting emotional literacy: anger management groups,' in N. Barwick (ed.) *Clinical Counselling in Schools.* London: Routledge

Simpson, L.J. (2016) *Into the Garden of Dreams.* Dunstable: Brilliant Publications

Stallard, P. (2002) *Think Good-Feel Good.* Chichester: John Wiley and Sons

Stallard, P. (2009) *Anxiety. Cognitive Behaviour Therapy with Children and Young People.* London and New York: Routledge

Stein, M.B. et al. (2008) 'Gene-by-environment.' *Neuropsychopharmacology,* 33, 312–319

Sunderland, M. (1997) *Draw on Your Emotions.* London: Routledge

Sunderland, M. & Armstrong N. (2001) *A Nifflenoo Called Nevermind.* London: Routledge

Sunderland, M. & Armstrong, N. (2001) *Willy and the Wobbly House: A Story for Children Who Are Anxious or Obsessional.* London: Routledge

Tolman, D., Impett, E., Tracy, A. & Michael, A. (2006) 'Looking good, sounding good: femininity, ideology and adolescent girls' mental health.' *Psychology of Women Quarterly,* 30, 85–95

Waldman, J. (2008) 'Narrowing the gap,' in *Local Government Association: Narrowing the Gap.* Available at: www.local.gov.uk

Warren, S. et al. (1997) 'Children's narrative representations of mothers: Their development and associations with child and mother adaptation.' *Journal of Child Development,* 68(1), 127–138

Wason, P.C. (1960) *Quarterly Journal of Experimental Psychology,* 12(3), 129–140

Wason, P.C. (1968) *Thinking and Reasoning.* Harmondsworth: Penguin

Webster, R. & Russell, A. (2015) *Maximising the Impact of Teaching Assistants.* London: Routledge

Wentzel, K.R. et al. (2004) 'Friendships in middle school.' *Journal of Educational Psychology,* 96, 195–203

Willets, C. & Creswell, L. (2012) *Overcoming Your Child's Fear and Worries.* London: Constable and Robinson

Useful websites

www.anxietyuk.org.uk – National British charity providing support and resources for parents and young people

www.bacp.co.uk/supervision – British Association of Counselling and Psychotherapy

www.barnardos.org.uk – Support for teenagers and primary aged children with anxiety

www.circle-time.co.uk/whole-school-approach – Jenny Mosley, circle time advice

www.corc.uk.net/outcome-experience-measures/revised-childrens-anxiety-and-depression-scale-and-subscales/ – RCADs resources and information

www.cwmt.org.uk – Charlie Waller Memorial Trust, resources for young people, parents, schools and colleges. For children and young people with mental health difficulties

www.faculty.londondeanery.ac.uk – London Deanery e-learning facility: supervision training and advice

www.gozen.com – Downloadable resources for parents and teachers

www.inourhands.com – Dr. Pooky Knightsmith, mental health educator

www.mendability.com – Sensory enrichment therapy

www.nhsinform.scot/healthy-living/food-and-nutrition/eating-well/eatwell-guide-how-to-eat-a-healthy-balanced-diet – Dietary advice

www.open.edu/openlearn/body-mind/childhood-youth/childhood-and-youth-studies/childhood/child-spirituality – Spirituality studies

www.pshe-association.org.uk – The national body for PSHE education

www.psychologytools.com – Psychology tools, resources for practitioners

www.st-andrews.ac.uk/students/advice/leaflets/examanxiety/ – Advice on managing exam anxiety

www.youngminds.org.uk – National British charity that supports parents and young people, helpline available

Index

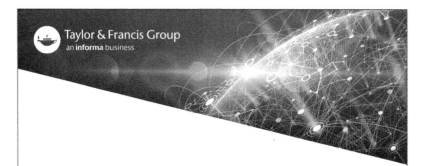